Designing & Teaching Learning Goals & Objectives

Robert J. Marzano

Marzano Research Laboratory
Powered by Solution Tree

THE **CLASSROOM** STRATEGIES **SERIES**

555 North Morton Street
Bloomington, IN 47404

888.849.0851
FAX: 866.801.1447

email: info@marzanoresearch.com
marzanoresearch.com

Visit **marzanoresearch.com/classroomstrategies** to download reproducibles from this book.

Printed in the United States of America

Library of Congress Control Number: 2009902837

ISBN: 978-0-9822592-0-7 (paperback)
         978-0-9822592-1-4 (library binding)

13 12 11   3 4 5

FSC
Mixed Sources
Product group from well-managed
forests and other controlled sources
Cert no. SW-COC-002283
www.fsc.org
© 1996 Forest Stewardship Council

Director of Production: Gretchen Knapp

Managing Editor of Production: Caroline Wise

Proofreader: Elisabeth Abrams

Text Designer: Amy Shock

Cover Designer: Pamela Rude

MARZANO RESEARCH LABORATORY DEVELOPMENT TEAM

Staff Writer

Lindsay A. Carleton

Marzano Research Laboratory Associates

Chris Briggs-Hale

Jane K. Doty Fischer

Maria C. Foseid

Mark P. Foseid

Tammy Heflebower

Edie Holcomb

Sharon Kramer

David Livingston

Beatrice McGarvey

Diane E. Paynter

Debra Pickering

Salle Quackenboss

Tom Roy

ACKNOWLEDGMENTS

Marzano Research Laboratory would like to thank the following reviewers:

Gloria Alter
Adjunct Associate Professor
Beloit College
Beloit, Wisconsin

Judy Beemer
Literacy Coach
Junction City High School
Junction City, Kansas

Heidi Legg Burros
Adjunct Assistant Professor
University of Arizona
Tucson, Arizona

Katy Lapp
Lecturer in Education and Supervisor for
    Secondary Student Teachers
Colorado College
Colorado Springs, Colorado

Baytoram Ramharack
Social Studies Department Chair and
    Teacher
Elmont Memorial High School
Elmont, New York

Sharon Roemer
Curriculum and Instruction Administrator
Lucia Mar Unified School District
Arroyo Grande, California

Marcia Sewall
Lecturer
University of California
San Diego, California

Heather Sparks
Eighth Grade Math Teacher
Taft Middle School
Oklahoma City, Oklahoma

Visit **marzanoresearch.com/classroomstrategies**
to download reproducibles from this book.

CONTENTS

Italicized entries indicate reproducible forms.

CHAPTER 3

DEVELOPING LEARNING GOALS AT DIFFERENT LEVELS OF DIFFICULTY IN THE SERVICE OF DIFFERENTIATION 25

CHAPTER 4

ORGANIZING LEARNING GOALS INTO A SCALE 63

CHAPTER 5

TEACHING IN A SYSTEM OF LEARNING GOALS 79

ABOUT THE AUTHOR

 Dr. Robert J. Marzano is the cofounder and CEO of Marzano Research Laboratory in Denver, Colorado. Throughout his forty years in the field of education, he has become a speaker, trainer, and author of more than thirty books and 150 articles on topics such as instruction, assessment, writing and implementing standards, cognition, effective leadership, and school intervention. His books include: *Designing and Assessing Educational Objectives, Making Standards Useful in the Classroom,* and *The Art and Science of Teaching.* His practical translations of the most current research and theory into classroom strategies are internationally known and widely practiced by both teachers and administrators. He received a bachelor's degree from Iona College in New York, a master's degree from Seattle University, and a doctorate from the University of Washington.

ABOUT MARZANO RESEARCH LABORATORY

Marzano Research Laboratory (MRL) is a joint venture between Solution Tree and Dr. Robert J. Marzano. MRL combines Dr. Marzano's forty years of educational research with continuous action research in all major areas of schooling in order to provide effective and accessible instructional strategies, leadership strategies, and classroom assessment strategies that are always at the forefront of best practice. By providing such an all-inclusive research-into-practice resource center, MRL provides teachers and principals the tools they need to effect profound and immediate improvement in student achievement.

INTRODUCTION

Designing and Teaching Learning Goals and Objectives is the first in a series of books collectively referred to as *The Classroom Strategies Series*. The purpose of this series is to provide classroom teachers and building and district administrators with an in-depth treatment of research-based instructional strategies that can be used in the classroom to enhance student achievement. Many of the strategies addressed in this series have been covered in other works such as *The Art and Science of Teaching: A Comprehensive Framework for Effective Instruction* (Marzano, 2007), *Classroom Management That Works* (Marzano, Marzano, & Pickering, 2003), and *Classroom Instruction That Works* (Marzano, Pickering, & Pollock, 2001). Although those works devoted a chapter or a part of a chapter to particular strategies, *The Classroom Strategies Series* devotes an entire book to an instructional strategy or set of related strategies.

Designing clear learning goals and objectives is a staple of effective teaching. We might even say that goal setting is a necessary condition for effective teaching. If teachers aren't sure of instructional goals, their instructional activities will not be focused, and unfocused instructional activities do not engender student learning. As straightforward as this might sound, designing and teaching goals and objectives takes insight into the nature of content and the nature of learning. *Designing and Teaching Learning Goals and Objectives* addresses the research, theory, and practice regarding the design and use of effective goals.

We begin with a brief but inclusive chapter that reviews the research and theory on goal setting. Although you might skip this chapter and move right into those that provide recommendations for classroom practice, you are strongly encouraged to examine the research and theory because it is the foundation for the entire book. Indeed, a basic purpose of *Designing and Teaching Learning Goals and Objectives* and others in *The Classroom Strategies Series* is to present the most useful instructional strategies that are based on the strongest research and theory available.

Because research and theory can provide only a general direction for classroom practice, *Designing and Teaching Learning Goals and Objectives* (and each book in the series) goes one step further to translate that research into specific applications for the classroom. It is important to note, however, that individual teachers must make necessary adaptations to meet the unique needs of their students.

How to Use This Book

Designing and Teaching Learning Goals and Objectives can be used as a self-study text that provides an in-depth understanding of how to design and teach classroom goals and objectives. As you progress through the chapters, you will encounter exercises. It is important to complete these exercises and then compare your answers with those in the back of the text. Such interaction provides a review of the content and allows you to examine how clearly you understand it.

Designing and Teaching Learning Goals and Objectives may also be used by teams of teachers or by an entire faculty who wishes to examine the topic of designing and teaching learning goals in depth. When this is the case, teacher teams should do the exercises independently and then compare their answers in small group and large group settings.

Chapter 1

RESEARCH AND THEORY

Before addressing the research and theory on goals and objectives, it is useful to consider the issue of terminology. The terms *goals* and *objectives* have been used by different people in different ways. For some, the term *goal* applies only to the overarching purpose of curriculum, and the term *objective* is reserved for day-to-day instructional targets. In the research and theoretical worlds, these terms tend to be used interchangeably for general and specific purposes. In this book, the terms will be used interchangeably. However, as the following discussion illustrates, the focus of this book is on day-to-day classroom instruction.

The importance of goals and objectives in education was established as far back as the first half of the last century by the educational philosopher and evaluation expert Ralph Tyler (1949a, 1949b). For Tyler, a well-constructed objective should contain a clear reference to a specific type of knowledge as well as reference to the behaviors that demonstrate proficiency relative to that knowledge. Prior to Tyler's recommendations, educators typically did not identify specific areas of information and skill as targets for student learning. Instead, broad topic areas such as "probability" or "World War II" represented the most specific level of curricular organization.

Where Tyler's insights into the nature of content and the nature of learning made it clear that educators must design specific objectives and identify the behaviors that demonstrate achievement of those objectives, David Krathwohl and David Payne (1971) made distinctions between three levels or types of objectives: global objectives, educational objectives, and instructional objectives. As described by Robert Marzano and John Kendall (2007), global objectives are the most general. They are broad, complex areas. For example, "Students will be able to apply basic properties of probability" would be considered a global objective.

Instructional objectives are the most specific of the three types of objectives. In *Preparing Instructional Objectives,* Robert Mager (1962) explained that a well-written instructional objective should include three elements:

1. **Performance.** An objective always says what a learner is expected to be able to do; the objective sometimes describes the product or result of the doing.

2. **Conditions.** An objective always describes the important conditions (if any) under which the performance is to occur.

3. **Criterion.** Whenever possible, an objective describes the criterion of acceptable performance by describing how well the learner must perform in order to be considered acceptable. (p. 21)

In the middle of the triad are educational objectives (Anderson et al., 2001). They articulate specific areas of knowledge, but don't identify the performance conditions and criteria for success as do instructional objectives. In *Designing and Teaching Learning Goals and Objectives*, we primarily address educational objectives, which we more commonly refer to as *learning goals*. How these goals can be addressed on the instructional level will also be examined in depth.

The importance of learning goals to the day-to-day execution of classroom activities is fairly obvious. Goals are the reason classroom activities are designed. Without clear goals, classroom activities are without direction. Researchers Joseph Krajcik, Katherine McNeill, and Brian Reiser (2007) explain that good teaching begins with clear learning goals from which teachers select appropriate instructional activities and assessments that help determine students' progress on the learning goals.

It is useful to keep in mind that goal setting is not unique to education. Indeed, it has its theoretical roots in organizational psychology. In their 1990 book *A Theory of Goal Setting and Task Performance*, Edwin Locke and Gary Latham provide an extensive history of goal-setting practice in the context of organizational theory. Although their research focus is exclusively on goal setting and performance in work settings, they note that much of the work-related goal theory can and should be extended to the field of education.

Table 1.1 (page 5) displays much of the research on which the recommendations in this book are based.

Dimensions of Learning Goals

From the research reported in table 1.1, one can conclude that two important characteristics of learning goals are *goal specificity* and *goal difficulty*. Goal specificity refers to the degree to which goals are defined in terms of clear and distinct outcomes. Goal difficulty refers to the degree to which goals provide a challenge to students.

Goal Specificity

Learning goals provide a set of shared expectations among students, teachers, administrators, and the general public. As discussed previously, they can range from the very specific (for example, "Students will be able to list the Great Lakes") to the very general ("Students will be able to write a well-formed essay"). The research strongly implies that the more specific the goals are, the better they are. That is, goals that are specific in nature are more strongly related to student achievement than goals that are not. For example, Mark Tubbs (1986) examined goal specificity in a meta-analysis of 48 studies in mostly organizational settings. He found an overall effect size of .50 for goal specificity, which supports the notion that more specific goals lead to higher achievement (see table 1.1).

The terms *meta-analysis* and *effect size* might be familiar to some readers and unfamiliar to others. (These terms and their relationship are described in some depth in appendix B on page 119.) Briefly, *meta-analysis* is a research technique for quantitatively synthesizing a series of studies on the same topic. In this case, Tubbs (1986) synthesized the findings of forty-eight studies on goal specificity. Typically, meta-analytic studies report their findings in terms of effect sizes (see the ES column in table 1.1). An *effect size* tells you how many standard deviations larger (or smaller) the average score for a group of

Table 1.1 Research Results for Goal Setting

Synthesis Study	Focus	Number of Effect Sizes (ESs)	Average ES	Percentile Gain
Wise & Okey, 1983[a]	General effects of setting goals or objectives	3	1.37	41
		25	.48	18
Chidester & Grigsby, 1984[b]	Goal difficulty	21	.44	17
Fuchs & Fuchs, 1985[b]	Long vs. short-term goals	96	.64	24
Tubbs, 1986[c]	Goal difficulty	56	.82	29
	Goal specificity	48	.50	19
	Goal setting and feedback	3	.56	21
	Participation in goal setting	17	.002	0
Mento, Steel, & Karren, 1987[b]	Goal difficulty	118	.58	22
Wood, Mento, & Locke, 1987[b]	Goal difficulty	72	.58	22
	Goal specificity	53	.43	17
Locke & Latham, 1990[c,d]	Goal difficulty	Not reported	.52–.82	20–29
	Goal specificity		.42–.80	16–29
Wright, 1990[b]	Goal difficulty	70	.55	21
Lipsey & Wilson, 1993	General effects of setting goals or objectives	204	.55	21
Kluger & DeNisi, 1996	Goal difficulty	37	.51	19
Utman, 1997	Mastery vs. performance goals	43	.53	20
Donovan & Radosevich, 1998[b]	Goal commitment	21	.36	14
Klein, Wesson, Hollenbeck, & Alge, 1999[b]	Goal commitment	83	.47	18
Hattie, 1999[e]	Goals and feedback	121	.46	18
Walberg, 1999	General effects of setting goals or objectives	21	.40	16
Burns, 2004[b]	Degree of challenge	45	.82	29
Gollwitzer & Sheeran, 2006[b]	Goal intentions on achievement	94	.72	26
Graham & Perin, 2007	Goal specificity	5	.70	26

[a] Two effect sizes are listed because of the manner in which effect sizes were reported. Readers should consult that study for more details.

[b] As reported in Hattie (2009).

[c] Both Tubbs (1986) and Locke and Latham (1990) report results from organizational as well as educational settings.

[d] As reported in Locke and Latham (2002).

[e] As reported in Hattie and Timperley (2007).

students who were exposed to a given strategy (in this case, highly specific goals) is than the average score for a group of students who were not exposed to a given strategy (in this case, nonspecific goals).

In short, an effect size tells you how powerful a strategy is; the larger the effect size, the more the strategy will increase student learning. Effect sizes are typically small numbers. In fact, the average effect size of most classroom strategies is .4 (Hattie, 2009). However, small effect sizes can translate into big percentage gains. For example, a strategy with an effect size of .4 translates into a 16 percentile point gain. This means that a student scoring at the 50th percentile in a class that did not use that strategy would be predicted to rise to the 66th percentile after the strategy had been introduced. (See appendix B, page 119, for a detailed description of effect sizes and a chart that translates effect size numbers into percentile gains.)

One of the more useful aspects of effect sizes is that they can be transformed into an expected percentile point gain (or loss) for the strategy under investigation. The effect size reported by Tubbs (1986) of .50 is associated with a 19 percentile point gain. Thus, taking the findings at face value, one could infer that an average student in a group of students who were provided with specific learning goals would be at the 69th percentile of a group of students who were exposed to very general learning goals. Another way of saying this is that a student at the 50th percentile in a class that used nonspecific goals (an average student in that group) would be predicted to rise to the 69th percentile if he or she were provided very specific learning goals. In short, goal specificity is an important element to consider when trying to enhance student achievement.

In their 1990 meta-analysis of organizational studies, Locke and Latham found effect sizes that ranged from .42–.80 for specific instead of general goals (translating to a 16–29 percentile point gain). They argued that specific goals provide more concrete guidance for achievement that more general goals lack. A lack of concrete guidance creates ambiguity that students in school and laborers in the workforce simply have trouble translating into specific expected behaviors. Specific goals provide a clear direction for behavior and a clear indication of desired performance, and as such they serve as motivators.

More recently, Steve Graham and Dolores Perin (2007) conducted a meta-analysis of achievement in writing. They found five studies relating to goal specificity. Examples of goal specificity used in their study included a clearly established purpose in a writing assignment and the specification of product expectations. They found an average effect size of .70 for goal specificity, which translates to a 26 percentile point gain. Accordingly, Graham and Perin (2007) concluded that "assigning product goals had a strong impact on writing quality" (p. 464), but warned that although their conclusion was based on high-quality studies, their findings were drawn from only five studies and so should be interpreted cautiously.

Goal Difficulty

Students will perceive learning goals as more or less difficult depending on their current state of knowledge, their beliefs about what causes achievement, and their perceptions of their own abilities. Studies indicate that students are most motivated by goals they perceive as difficult but not too difficult. For example, Tubbs (1986) found an average effect size of .82 for difficult versus easy goals (translating to a 29 percentile point gain). The Locke and Latham (1990) meta-analysis found effect sizes of .52–.82 for difficult goals (a 20–29 percentile point gain), noting that "performance leveled off or decreased only when the limits of ability were reached or when commitment to a highly difficult goal lapsed" (p. 706). Goal difficulty may also moderate or change the effect of feedback on student achievement. For example, Avraham Kluger and Angelo DeNisi (1996) found that feedback as an instructional strategy is more effective when learning goals are at the right level of difficulty—challenging, but not too difficult.

Types of Learning Goals

In addition to their specificity and difficulty, learning goals vary in terms of their purposes and functions. Learning goals that emphasize mastery of content, or *mastery goals*, might enhance learning more than goals that specify attainment of a specific score, or *performance goals*. *Noncognitive* goals that involve students in cooperative tasks might have a unique effect of their own.

Mastery vs. Performance Goals

One well-investigated distinction regarding learning goals involves their overarching purpose; namely, mastery or performance. The first type, mastery goals, focuses on *developing* competence. The second type, performance goals, focuses on *demonstrating* competence by obtaining a specific score or grade (Kaplan, Middleton, Urdan, & Midgley, 2001).

This distinction between mastery goals and performance goals is subtle but profound in its implications. Performance goals will typically include a desired score or grade. For example, the following would be considered performance goals:

Students will obtain a grade of B or higher by the end of the grading period.

All students will be determined proficient or higher in reading by the end of the school year.

As these examples illustrate, performance goals don't describe content as much as they do a specific score or grade. Mastery goals, by definition, articulate the content that is to be learned. For example, the following are mastery goals:

Students will be able to use word segmentation and syllables to decode an unrecognized word.

Students will be able to compare ordinal numbers through the fifth position (that is, 1st, 2nd, 3rd, 4th, 5th).

Although each type of goal may be associated with increased student achievement, research indicates that mastery goals are typically associated with higher order learning and better retention than are performance goals, especially for more challenging content. For example, in his meta-analysis, Christopher Utman (1997) found an average effect size of .53 (a 20 percentile point gain) for mastery versus performance goals for grade school students completing a complex task. Research by Judith Meece (1991) revealed that teachers who used mastery goals in their classrooms promoted more meaningful learning, provided more developmentally appropriate instruction, and supported student autonomy more than did teachers with performance-oriented classrooms.

Noncognitive Goals

Much of the research on goals over the decades has focused on academic goals, sometimes referred to as *cognitive* goals. However, attention to *noncognitive* goals in education has increased in recent years. For example, a 2005 issue of *Educational Assessment* was devoted to noncognitive goals. In their introduction to the volume, editors Jamal Abedi and Harold F. O'Neil noted that "the affective (feeling) and psychomotor (doing) issues affect cognitive performance and are worthwhile domains of learning themselves" (p. 147). The remainder of the volume focused on the role of noncognitive goals such as motivation and affect in education.

Joseph Durlak and Roger Weissberg (2007) investigated the effects of after-school programs on noncognitive goals such as students' personal and social skills. They limited their analysis to programs that used "evidence-based" instructional strategies, which they defined as "well-sequenced" and "active." Relative to well-sequenced, Durlak and Weissberg noted:

> New skills cannot be acquired immediately. It takes time and effort to develop new behaviors and often more complicated skills must be broken down into smaller steps and sequentially mastered. Therefore, a coordinated sequence of activities is required that links the learning steps and provides youth with opportunities to connect these steps. Usually, this occurs through lesson plans or program manuals, particularly if programs use or adapt established criteria. (p. 10)

About active forms of learning, they noted:

> Active forms of learning require youth to act on the material. That is, after youth receive some basic instruction they should then have the opportunity to practice new behaviors and receive feedback on their performance. This is accomplished through role playing and other types of behavioral rehearsal strategies, and the cycle of practice and feedback continues until mastery is achieved. These hands-on forms of learning are much preferred over exclusively didactic instruction, which rarely translates into behavioral change. (p. 10)

After examining ten studies that met their criterion of using evidence-based strategies, they concluded that after-school programs reduced problem behaviors and contributed significantly to student achievement and positive self-concept.

Durlak and Weissberg's study is noteworthy because it demonstrates that noncognitive goals can be a viable instructional focus. It is also noteworthy because it supports the linkage between noncognitive goals and achievement outcomes. Their meta-analysis found that effective after-school programs produced a positive impact on participating students' academic achievement with an effect size of .31, which translates to a 12 percentile point gain.

Jeff Valentine, David DuBois, and Harris Cooper (2004) conducted a meta-analysis that sheds light on the importance of noncognitive goals. They examined the effects of self-beliefs on student achievement. They synthesized the results of studies that measured student academic achievement and self-beliefs at an initial point and then again at a later point. They found that positive student self-beliefs had a small but significant influence (an effect size of .16 over 60 studies) on subsequent student achievement. Valentine et al. note that noncognitive goals that address students' self-beliefs are most effective when tailored to the content being taught. For example, noncognitive goals regarding beliefs about mathematics (let's say) have a stronger effect on achievement in mathematics than noncognitive goals regarding beliefs about academics in general.

Cooperative Learning and Noncognitive Goals

When considering noncognitive goals, one must consider cooperative learning as a necessary instructional component. Cooperative learning has a rich body of research in its own right. Cary Roseth, David Johnson, and Roger Johnson (2008) used a model based in social interdependence theory to investigate the relationship between cooperative goal structures and student achievement and peer relations in adolescent students, updating and elaborating on their earlier meta-analyses (Johnson & Johnson, 1989; Johnson, Maruyama, Johnson, Nelson, & Skon, 1981). They characterized cooperative goal structures as those involving "positive interdependence." This means that they involve linked positive outcomes, mutually beneficial actions, and sharing of resources. Roseth, Johnson, and Johnson (2008) found that cooperative goal structures involving positive interdependence had a stronger relationship with achievement than did competitive or individualistic goal structures (average effect sizes .57 and .65, respectively). They concluded:

> By implication, this study suggests that the more early adolescents' teachers structure students' academic goals cooperatively (as opposed to competitively or individualistically), (a) the more students will tend to achieve, (b) the more positive students' relationships will tend to be, and (c) the more higher levels of achievement will be associated with more positive peer relationships. (p. 237)

Taking this research at face value, it would be easy to conclude that cooperative goal structures are superior to other forms of goal structure regardless of the type of goal being addressed—cognitive or noncognitive. Witness the impressive results reported in table 1.2 (page 10) by David Johnson, Geoffrey Maruyama, Roger Johnson, Deborah Nelson, and Linda Skon (1981) for cooperative learning versus individual student competition (an effect size of .78 in favor of cooperative learning) and cooperative learning versus individual student tasks (an effect size of .78 in favor of cooperative learning). However, the actual practice of cooperative learning leans more toward a focus on noncognitive goals. This is demonstrated in the literature that describes how teachers might implement cooperative learning in their classrooms, such as *Cooperation in the Classroom* (Johnson, Johnson, & Holubec, 1998) and *Learning Together and Alone: Cooperative, Competitive, and Individualistic Learning* (Johnson & Johnson, 1999). In *Learning Together and Alone,* Roger Johnson and David Johnson make the following distinction:

> A learning goal is a desired future state of demonstrating competence or mastery in the subject area being studied. The **goal structure** specifies the ways in which students will interact with each other and the teacher to achieve the goal. Students may interact to promote each other's success or obstruct each other's success. Students may also avoid interaction and thereby have no effect on the success or failure of others. Whenever people strive to achieve a goal, they may engage in cooperative, competitive, or individualistic efforts. (p. 3, emphasis in original)

This clears up much of the potential confusion regarding the literature on cooperative goal structures. Cooperative *goals* are not established in lieu of individual goals. Instead, cooperative goal *structures* are established to help students accomplish academic goals. Individual students are still held accountable for accomplishing academic goals, but those individual students do not have to work in isolation or in competition to accomplish those goals. Additionally, cooperative structures are particularly useful when focusing on noncognitive goals because cooperative learning skills are commonly the very targets of many noncognitive goals.

Another perspective on the power of cooperative goal structures to enhance noncognitive goals was highlighted by Marika Ginsburg-Block, Cynthia Rohrbeck, and John Fantuzzo (2006). They conducted a meta-analysis on the effects of peer-assisted learning on elementary school students' social skills, self-concept, and behavior. They found effect sizes of .52, .40, and .65 for noncognitive goals

Table 1.2 Research Results for Cooperative Learning

Synthesis Study	Focus	Number of Effect Sizes (ESs)	Average ES	Percentile Gain
Johnson, Maruyama, Johnson, Nelson, & Skon, 1981	Cooperative learning (general)	122	.73	27
	Cooperative vs. intergroup competition	9	.00	0
	Cooperative vs. individual competition	70	.78	28
	Cooperative vs. individual student tasks	104	.78	28
Hall, 1989	Cooperative learning (general)	37	.30	12
Lipsey & Wilson, 1993	Cooperative learning (general)	414	.63	24
Walberg, 1999	Cooperative learning (general)	182	.78	28
Bowen, 2000	Cooperative learning (general), high school and college chemistry	30	.37	14
Haas, 2005	Cooperative learning (general)	3	.34	13
Ginsburg-Block, Rohrbeck, & Fantuzzo, 2006	Peer-assisted learning on social skills	30	.52	20
	Peer-assisted learning on self-concept	15	.40	16
	Peer-assisted learning on behavior	12	.65	24
Durlak & Weissberg, 2007	After-school programs	10	.31	12
Roseth, Johnson, & Johnson, 2008	Cooperative vs. competitive goals	13	.57	22
	Cooperative vs. individualistic goals	40	.65	24

involving social skills, self-concept, and behavior, respectively (translating to 20, 16, and 24 percentile point gains). Table 1.2 reports much of the research on cooperative learning.

Communicating Goals and Providing Feedback

If goals provide clear targets for learning, then feedback may be thought of as information that facilitates the process of reaching those targets. Researchers John Hattie and Helen Timperley (2007) claim that in educational settings "the main purpose of feedback is to reduce discrepancies between current understandings and performance and a goal" (p. 86). Their comprehensive review synthesized research on the power of feedback to improve student achievement. Noting that many of the individual findings included in feedback meta-analyses are negative (showing that feedback sometimes inhibits performance), Hattie and Timperley distinguished between the effects of feedback about the task, the process, self-regulation, and the self. Feedback regarding the task, process, and self-regulation is often effective, whereas feedback regarding the self (often delivered as praise) typically does not enhance learning and achievement. They concluded:

> Learning can be enhanced to the degree that students share the challenging goals of learning, adopt self-assessment and evaluation strategies, and develop error detection procedures and heightened self-efficacy to tackle more challenging tasks leading to mastery and understanding of lessons. (p. 103).

Table 1.3 presents the findings regarding feedback for a number of meta-analytic studies. Based on the findings reported in the table, one can conclude that feedback should be an integral part of any teacher's arsenal of strategies. Within *The Classroom Strategies Series*, we highlight the research on feedback in the book *Formative Assessment and Standards-Based Grading* (Marzano, in press). Here we include the research on feedback because it has a symbiotic relationship with goals. Without effective goals, feedback is impossible. Without feedback, goals are rendered quite sterile.

Table 1.3 Research Results for Feedback

Synthesis Study	Focus	Number of Effect Sizes (ESs)	Average ES	Percentile Gain
Bloom, 1976	General effects of feedback	8	1.47	43
Lysakowski & Walberg, 1981[a]	General effects of feedback	39	1.15	37
Lysakowski & Walberg, 1982	General effects of feedback	94	.97	33
Yeany & Miller, 1983[a]	Diagnostic feedback in science	49	.52	20
Moin, 1986[a]	General effects of feedback		.29	11
Haller, Child, & Walberg, 1998[b]	General effects of feedback	115	.71	26
Tenenbaum & Goldring, 1989	General effects of feedback	16	.66	25
Bangert-Drowns, Kulik, Kulik, & Morgan, 1991	General effects of feedback	58	.26	10
Kumar, 1991[c]	General effects of feedback	5	1.35	41
Azevedo & Bernard, 1995	Immediate feedback in computer-based instruction	22	.80	29
Kluger & DeNisi, 1996[a]	Effects of feedback interventions	607	.41	16
Walberg, 1999	General effects of feedback	20	.94	33
Hattie, 1999[a]	General effects of feedback	74	.95	33
Haas, 2005	General effects of feedback	19	.55	21

[a] As reported in Hattie & Timperley, 2007.

[b] Feedback was embedded in general metacognitive strategies.

[c] The dependant variable was engagement.

What can a teacher take away from the research? Certainly one generalization is that setting clear and specific goals for learning that are at just the right level of difficulty can greatly enhance student achievement.

Translating Research Into Classroom Practice

In subsequent chapters, we will translate the research presented in this chapter into a number of recommendations for designing learning goals and the tasks that determine accomplishment of those goals. As mentioned in the introduction, as you progress through the remaining chapters, you will encounter exercises that ask you to examine the content presented. Some of these exercises ask you to answer specific questions. Answer these questions in the space provided, and check your answers with those reported in the back of the book. Other exercises are more open-ended and ask you to generate applications of what you have read. Reproducible versions of the exercises are included at the end of each chapter, and reproducible answer sheets are included at the end of the book. Visit **marzanoresearch .com/classroomstrategies** to download all the exercises and answers in this book.

Chapter 2

DEVELOPING SPECIFIC LEARNING GOALS AND TASKS

In chapter 1, we saw that goal specificity is an important aspect of designing effective goals. In general, specific goals have a more powerful effect on student achievement than do general goals. Goal specificity begins with making a distinction between learning goals and the classroom activities and assignments that will support those goals. Stated differently, there is often confusion between goals, activities, and assignments. For example, consider the following list. It typifies what you might find in the learning goals section of some teachers' planning books.

1. Students will successfully complete the exercises in the back of chapter 3.

2. Students will create a metaphor representing the food pyramid.

3. Students will be able to determine subject/verb agreement in a variety of simple, compound, and complete sentences.

4. Students will understand the defining characteristics of fables, fairy tales, and tall tales.

5. Students will investigate the relationship between speed of air flow and lift provided by an airplane wing.

Statements 1, 2, and 5 are activities or assignments. As the names imply, *activities* and *assignments* are things students will be asked to *do*. They are a critical part of effective teaching, but they are not ends in themselves. They constitute the means by which the ends, or learning goals, are to be accomplished.

By contrast, statements 3 and 4 are learning goals. A *learning goal* is a statement of what students will know or be able to do. Note that statements 3 and 4 begin with "Students will be able to" and "Students will understand," respectively. Activities and assignments are stated in less-structured ways. To illustrate, the second column of table 2.1 (page 14) lists learning goals for science, language arts, mathematics, and social studies along with related activities or assignments in the third column.

Typically, students complete activities with guidance and help from the teacher and complete assignments independently. There is certainly overlap in these categories of behaviors. However, the mathematics example in table 2.1 would most likely be an assignment; the science, language arts, and social studies examples would most likely be activities. Exercise 2.1 provides some

Table 2.1 Learning Goals and Activities/Assignments

Subject	Learning Goals	Activities/Assignments
Science	Students will understand: • The sun is the largest body in the solar system. • The moon and earth rotate on their axes. • The moon orbits the earth while the earth orbits the sun.	Students will watch the video on the relationship between the earth and the moon and the place of these bodies in the solar system.
Language arts	Students will be able to: • Sound out words that are not in their sight vocabulary but are known to them.	Students will observe the teacher modeling sounding and blending strategies.
Mathematics	Students will be able to: • Solve equations with one variable.	Students will practice solving 10 equations in cooperative groups.
Social studies	Students will understand: • The defining characteristics of the barter system.	Students will describe what the United Sates might be like if it were based on the barter system as opposed to a monetary system.

practice in differentiating between learning goals and activities and assignments. (See page 21 for a reproducible of this exercise and page 98 for a reproducible answer sheet. Visit **marzanoresearch .com/classroomstrategies** to download all the exercises and answers in this book.)

Exercise 2.1
Learning Goals vs. Activities and Assignments

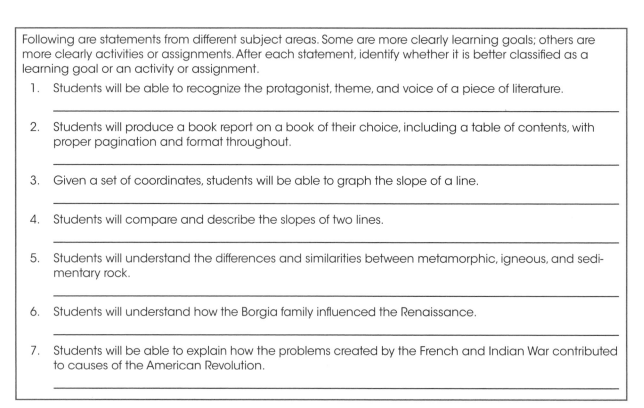

Following are statements from different subject areas. Some are more clearly learning goals; others are more clearly activities or assignments. After each statement, identify whether it is better classified as a learning goal or an activity or assignment.

1. Students will be able to recognize the protagonist, theme, and voice of a piece of literature.

    _____

2. Students will produce a book report on a book of their choice, including a table of contents, with proper pagination and format throughout.

    _____

3. Given a set of coordinates, students will be able to graph the slope of a line.

    _____

4. Students will compare and describe the slopes of two lines.

    _____

5. Students will understand the differences and similarities between metamorphic, igneous, and sedimentary rock.

    _____

6. Students will understand how the Borgia family influenced the Renaissance.

    _____

7. Students will be able to explain how the problems created by the French and Indian War contributed to causes of the American Revolution.

    _____

8. Students will produce a play dramatizing the problems created by the French and Indian War and how they contributed to causes of the American Revolution.

   _____

9. Students will understand that matter is made up of atoms and that atoms, in turn, are made up of subatomic particles.

   _____

10. Students will write a paper describing the relationships among atoms and subatomic particles.

    _____

Think in Terms of Two Types of Goals

When first learning how to set specific goals, we recommend that you state them in one of the following two formats:

Students will be able to _____ .

Students will understand _____ .

The reason for the two formats is that content knowledge can be organized into two broad categories: declarative knowledge and procedural knowledge (Anderson et al., 2001; Marzano & Kendall, 2007). Chapter 3 addresses these two types of knowledge in some depth. Briefly, *declarative knowledge* is informational. *Procedural knowledge* involves skills, strategies, and processes. In table 2.1, the learning goals for science and social studies are declarative, or informational. Hence they employ the stem, "Students will understand." The mathematics and language arts goals are procedural or strategy-oriented. Hence they employ the stem, "Students will be able to." Occasionally, a learning goal involves a substantial amount of declarative and procedural knowledge. In such cases a useful format is the following:

Students will understand _____ and be able to _____ .

To illustrate, the following is a learning goal for a topic regarding number sense at the third grade level that includes both declarative and procedural knowledge:

Students will understand the defining characteristics of whole numbers, decimals, and fractions with like denominators, and will be able to convert between equivalent forms as well as represent factors and multiples of whole numbers through 100.

The distinction between declarative and procedural knowledge is important and should be kept in mind when designing learning goals. Sometimes it is fairly easy to discern declarative versus procedural knowledge. For example, consider a goal that involves computing the area of a triangle. This is basically a procedure in that it involves a set of steps that students must execute: they must multiply the length of the base by the height and then take one-half of that product. Likewise, consider a goal that involves knowing the state capitals. This is clearly declarative in that it involves knowledge of information. However, now consider a goal that involves decimals. Depending on the teacher's approach, the focus could be procedural or declarative. If the instructional focus is an understanding of important characteristics of decimals (such as the value of places to the right of the decimal point), then the goal is declarative in nature. However, if the focus is on converting between fractions and decimals, then the goal is procedural in nature. Exercise 2.2 provides some practice in identifying declarative versus procedural knowledge. (See page 22 for a reproducible of this exercise and page 100 for a reproducible answer sheet. Visit **marzanoresearch.com/classroomstrategies** to download all the exercises and answers in this book.)

Exercise 2.2
Declarative vs. Procedural Knowledge

Following are ten statements regarding academic content. For each one, determine whether it is declarative, procedural, or either. If either, explain why.

1.	Creating a line graph to represent data	Declarative	Procedural	Either
2.	Describing the events that led to the Cold War	Declarative	Procedural	Either
3.	Determining breathing rate and heart rate	Declarative	Procedural	Either
4.	Refusal skills	Declarative	Procedural	Either
5.	Characteristics of chance events	Declarative	Procedural	Either
6.	Keyboarding techniques	Declarative	Procedural	Either
7.	Keeping in rhythm	Declarative	Procedural	Either
8.	The relationship between the seasons and the tilt of the earth	Declarative	Procedural	Either
9.	Survey sampling technique	Declarative	Procedural	Either
10.	Front-end rounding	Declarative	Procedural	Either

One final comment should be made about use of the phrases "Students will understand" and "Students will be able to." Some educators object to the use of the verb *understand* in goal statements on the grounds that it is inappropriate and nonspecific. The first part of this criticism is inaccurate. The verb *understand* is entirely appropriate when designing declarative goals. The second part of the criticism is accurate. It is not very specific in that it does not describe how students are to demonstrate their understanding. In the next section and following, you will see that we set aside the convention of using the verb *understand* with declarative goals and use more specific verbs such as *describe*, *explain*, and the like. You will also note that we sometimes use the phrase "will be able to" with declarative goals: "Students will be able to explain the defining characteristics of the cell membrane." This relaxing of the syntactic rules for stating declarative and procedural goals described is completely appropriate once a teacher has a firm grasp of the distinction between the two types. In the beginning, however, we recommend the use of two different formats to explicitly mark declarative and procedural goals.

Exercise 2.2 typifies a problem frequently encountered by classroom teachers; they are provided with very general statements regarding content knowledge that must be translated into specific learning goals to be useful instructionally. This problem is all too common when working with state standards documents, district curriculum documents, or district- or school-designed lists of essential learner outcomes. To illustrate, table 2.2 contains typical general statements found in such documents.

Table 2.2 Typical Statements Found in State and District Standards Documents and Essential Learner Outcomes

Subject and Grade Level	Statement
Social studies 6–8	Understands the basic concept of a democracy
Language arts 3–5	Understands and uses a variety of sentence types
Math 6–8	Understands and applies the concept of functions
Science 5–7	Understands the concept of natural selection
Physical education 3–5	Demonstrates defensive skills in softball
Art 1–3	Understands and applies basic principles of primary and secondary colors
Music 6–8	Improvises simple melodies

The statements in the right column of table 2.2 provide some guidance as to what students are expected to know or be able to do, but not enough. An effective learning goal provides students (and the teacher) with a clear understanding of the target knowledge. *Target knowledge* can be defined as the information and/or skill, strategy, or process that demonstrates attainment of the learning goal.

To translate general statements like those found in table 2.2 into learning goals, a teacher must articulate the more specific declarative or procedural knowledge implied in the general statement. For example, consider the general statement for social studies in table 2.2: "Understands the basic concept of a democracy." Implied in this general statement is that the students will understand specific defining characteristics of democracies. This would be explicitly articulated in a learning goal such as the following:

> Students will be able to explain the basic defining characteristics of a democracy, including the following:
>
> > Civic responsibility is exercised by voting, and power is exercised through elected representatives.
> >
> > Majority is rule, and there is a focus on individual rights.
> >
> > Governments exist at regional and local levels so they can be as accessible to the people as possible.

Notice that this statement uses the phrase "will be able to" along with a specific verb (*explain*) in a goal statement. As mentioned in the previous section, this format (and many others) is appropriate once you develop the awareness that the focus of this learning goal is declarative knowledge—in this case, information about the defining characteristics of democracy. The intent of the goal is that the students "understand" these characteristics. The vehicle they will use to demonstrate their understanding is explaining.

Now consider the general statement in table 2.2 for language arts: "Understands and uses a variety of sentence types." Implied in this statement is that students will understand different sentence types (simple, compound, complex) and be able to generate these types when writing an essay. A learning goal that might be designed from this general statement is:

> Students will be able to produce examples of simple, compound, and complex sentences and write a brief essay that includes all three types.

As the social studies and language arts examples illustrate, constructing learning goals from general statements involves knowing or inferring the intent of the authors of the general statement. Stated differently, a teacher must rely on his or her knowledge of the expectations for students at specific grade levels and in specific content areas to translate general statements into specific learning goals. This is sometimes as much art as it is science. Exercise 2.3 provides some practice. (See page 23 for a reproducible of this exercise and page 102 for a reproducible answer sheet. Visit **marzanoresearch .com/classroomstrategies** to download all the exercises and answers in this book.)

Exercise 2.3
Translating General Statements Into Learning Goals

Following are phrases representing general aspects of information and skill in specific subject areas. Translate these phrases into clearer statements of learning goals. For example, if you are provided with the phrase "writing effective paragraphs," you might translate this into the goal statement: "Students will be able to write paragraphs that include clear transition statements from one paragraph to the next."

The idea behind this exercise is to write learning goals that provide more specific guidance for the student and the teacher.

1. Language arts general statement: Speaking effectively

   Goal statement:

2. Mathematics general statement: Reducing fractions

   Goal statement:

3. Science general statement: Understanding photosynthesis

   Goal statement:

4. Social studies general statement: Knowing local history

   Goal statement:

5. Physical education general statement: Agility

   Goal statement:

6. Technology general statement: Using Excel

   Goal statement:

7. World languages general statement: Spanish conversation

   Goal statement:

8. The arts general statement: Music appreciation

   Goal statement:

9. Language arts general statement: Reading comprehension

   Goal statement:

10. Mathematics general statement: Estimating

    Goal statement:

    Now write a specific learning goal for your own subject area:

Design Tasks to Accompany Learning Goals

After a teacher has articulated a clear learning goal, the next logical step is to design a task or tasks that will be used to determine whether students have accomplished that particular goal. Designing tasks to accompany learning goals makes expectations for students even more specific. To illustrate, consider the following learning goal requiring procedural knowledge in mathematics:

> Students will be able to solve routine problems involving perimeter.

To determine whether students can accomplish this goal, a teacher might design a task like the following:

> If the earth's diameter is 12,740 km, what is the circumference? Show how you solved this problem.

The example involving perimeter is procedural. It requires students to execute a process—that of computing the perimeter. Now consider the following science goal that is more declarative in nature:

> Students will be able to provide examples that demonstrate the law of unbalanced forces.

The following task could be used to determine whether students met this goal:

> We have been studying the generalization that whenever an object speeds up or slows down, an unbalanced force has acted on it. Describe three examples of this generalization.

As we shall see in subsequent chapters, a system of well-constructed tasks to accompany learning goals provides a powerful framework for curriculum and assessment. Well-structured learning goals make assessment tasks easier to construct, and well-constructed assessment tasks help operationalize learning goals. Table 2.3 provides further examples of learning goals and their related assessment tasks.

Table 2.3 Learning Goals and Assessment Tasks

Subject Area	Learning Goal	Assessment Task
Language arts	Students will be able to use syllabication to sound out words.	Break each of the words below into syllables using the format provided, and then put the syllables back together to sound out the word.
Math	Students will be able to find the volume of a cylinder given its circumference and height.	The cylinder in the drawing below has a circumference of 42 cm and a height of 26 cm. Find the volume of the cylinder, showing your work.
Social studies	Students will describe the major events of the Vietnam War and the order in which they occurred.	Create a timeline that orders the following events: the Gulf of Tonkin Resolution, the Battle of the Ia Drang, and the Tet Offensive. In the space provided, briefly explain the significance of each event.
Science	Students will describe the key characteristics of warm-blooded animals (internal maintenance of temperature, live births).	From the group of pictures of animals provided, select an animal that is warm-blooded. Briefly explain what makes the animal warm-blooded and what excludes another animal from the same group.

Exercise 2.4 provides some practice in designing assessment tasks for learning goals. (See page 24 for a reproducible of this exercise and page 104 for a reproducible answer sheet. Visit **marzanoresearch .com/classroomstrategies** to download all the exercises and answers in this book.)

Exercise 2.4
Designing Assessment Tasks for Learning Goals

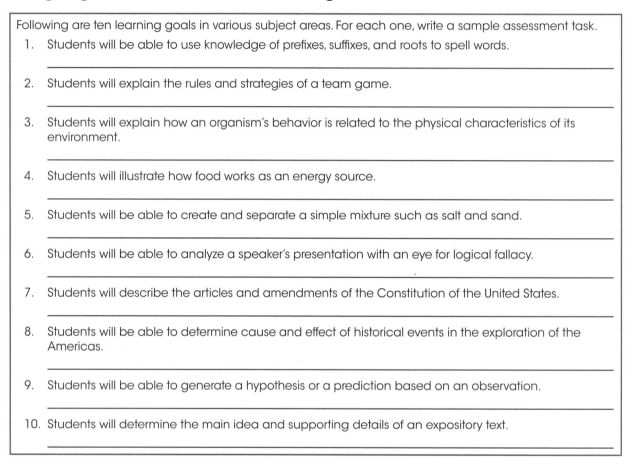

Following are ten learning goals in various subject areas. For each one, write a sample assessment task.

1. Students will be able to use knowledge of prefixes, suffixes, and roots to spell words.

2. Students will explain the rules and strategies of a team game.

3. Students will explain how an organism's behavior is related to the physical characteristics of its environment.

4. Students will illustrate how food works as an energy source.

5. Students will be able to create and separate a simple mixture such as salt and sand.

6. Students will be able to analyze a speaker's presentation with an eye for logical fallacy.

7. Students will describe the articles and amendments of the Constitution of the United States.

8. Students will be able to determine cause and effect of historical events in the exploration of the Americas.

9. Students will be able to generate a hypothesis or a prediction based on an observation.

10. Students will determine the main idea and supporting details of an expository text.

Summary

This chapter began with the distinction between learning goals and activities and assignments. Learning goals are the ends, and activities and assignments are the means to those ends. When designing learning goals, it is useful to keep in mind that distinction between declarative knowledge (information) and procedural knowledge (skills, strategies, and processes). Sometimes a teacher must translate general statements from standards documents into more specific goals. After developing a clear learning goal, construct a task or tasks that will help determine whether students have attained the learning goal.

Exercise 2.1

Learning Goals vs. Activities and Assignments

Following are statements from different subject areas. Some are more clearly learning goals; others are more clearly activities or assignments. After each statement, identify whether it is better classified as a learning goal or an activity or assignment.

1. Students will be able to recognize the protagonist, theme, and voice of a piece of literature.

   _____

2. Students will produce a book report on a book of their choice, including a table of contents, with proper pagination and format throughout.

   _____

3. Given a set of coordinates, students will be able to graph the slope of a line.

   _____

4. Students will compare and describe the slopes of two lines.

   _____

5. Students will understand the differences and similarities between metamorphic, igneous, and sedimentary rock.

   _____

6. Students will understand how the Borgia family influenced the Renaissance.

   _____

7. Students will be able to explain how the problems created by the French and Indian War contributed to causes of the American Revolution.

   _____

8. Students will produce a play dramatizing the problems created by the French and Indian War and how they contributed to causes of the American Revolution.

   _____

9. Students will understand that matter is made up of atoms and that atoms, in turn, are made up of subatomic particles.

   _____

10. Students will write a paper describing the relationships among atoms and subatomic particles.

    _____

Exercise 2.2

Declarative vs. Procedural Knowledge

Following are ten statements regarding academic content. For each one, determine whether it is declarative, procedural, or either. If either, explain why.

1. Creating a line graph to represent data   Declarative   Procedural   Either

   _____

2. Describing the events that led to the Cold War   Declarative   Procedural   Either

   _____

3. Determining breathing rate and heart rate   Declarative   Procedural   Either

   _____

4. Refusal skills   Declarative   Procedural   Either

   _____

5. Characteristics of chance events   Declarative   Procedural   Either

   _____

6. Keyboarding techniques   Declarative   Procedural   Either

   _____

7. Keeping in rhythm   Declarative   Procedural   Either

   _____

8. The relationship between the seasons and the tilt of the earth   Declarative   Procedural   Either

   _____

9. Survey sampling technique   Declarative   Procedural   Either

   _____

10. Front-end rounding   Declarative   Procedural   Either

    _____

Exercise 2.3

Translating General Statements Into Learning Goals

Following are phrases representing general aspects of information and skill in specific subject areas. Translate these phrases into clearer statements of learning goals. For example, if you are provided with the phrase "writing effective paragraphs," you might translate this into the goal statement: "Students will be able to write paragraphs that include clear transition statements from one paragraph to the next."

The idea behind this exercise is to write learning goals that provide more specific guidance for the student and the teacher.

1. Language arts general statement: Speaking effectively
   Goal statement:

2. Mathematics general statement: Reducing fractions
   Goal statement:

3. Science general statement: Understanding photosynthesis
   Goal statement:

4. Social studies general statement: Knowing local history
   Goal statement:

5. Physical education general statement: Agility
   Goal statement:

6. Technology general statement: Using Excel
   Goal statement:

7. World languages general statement: Spanish conversation
   Goal statement:

8. The arts general statement: Music appreciation
   Goal statement:

9. Language arts general statement: Reading comprehension
   Goal statement:

10. Mathematics general statement: Estimating
    Goal statement:

    Now write a specific learning goal for your own subject area:

Exercise 2.4

Designing Assessment Tasks for Learning Goals

Following are ten learning goals in various subject areas. For each one, write a sample assessment task.

1. Students will be able to use knowledge of prefixes, suffixes, and roots to spell words.

   _____

2. Students will explain the rules and strategies of a team game.

   _____

3. Students will explain how an organism's behavior is related to the physical characteristics of its environment.

   _____

4. Students will illustrate how food works as an energy source.

   _____

5. Students will be able to create and separate a simple mixture such as salt and sand.

   _____

6. Students will be able to analyze a speaker's presentation with an eye for logical fallacy.

   _____

7. Students will describe the articles and amendments of the Constitution of the United States.

   _____

8. Students will be able to determine cause and effect of historical events in the exploration of the Americas.

   _____

9. Students will be able to generate a hypothesis or a prediction based on an observation.

   _____

10. Students will determine the main idea and supporting details of an expository text.

    _____

Chapter 3

DEVELOPING LEARNING GOALS AT DIFFERENT LEVELS OF DIFFICULTY IN THE SERVICE OF DIFFERENTIATION

In chapter 1 on research and theory, we saw that goals should be at the right difficulty level to enhance student achievement. They can't be too easy, or they will bore students. They can't be too difficult, or they will frustrate students. Instead, they must challenge students but be perceived as attainable.

In a classroom with twenty-five or more students, developing learning goals at the right level of difficulty can pose significant obstacles for teachers. Given that students will be at different levels of understanding or skill in terms of the content being studied, how can a teacher write a goal for all students that satisfies the criterion "challenging but attainable"? The answer is fairly straightforward. For a given topic in a unit of instruction, construct goals at multiple levels of difficulty.

To a great extent, this chapter provides a framework for differentiation. Carol Ann Tomlinson's work in books such as *The Differentiated Classroom: Responding to the Needs of All Learners* (Tomlinson, 1999) and *How to Differentiate Instruction in Mixed-Ability Classrooms* (Tomlinson, 2004) has demonstrated the importance of differentiating instruction in a class to meet the diverse needs of students in the class. From the perspective of this book, differentiating begins with designing learning goals at different levels of difficulty.

In this chapter, we present a framework or *taxonomy* for writing goals at differing levels of difficulty. That taxonomy is articulated in depth in two related books: *The New Taxonomy of Educational Objectives* (Marzano & Kendall, 2007) and *Designing and Assessing Educational Objectives: Applying the New Taxonomy* (Marzano & Kendall, 2008). Table 3.1 (page 26) presents learning goals and tasks at four levels of difficulty from the New Taxonomy.

In table 3.1, the general topic is the solar system. Four objectives representing four levels of difficulty have been written for this topic. The first level requires students to simply recognize or recall important details. This is the least demanding of the learning goals. The second level requires students to explain critical features of the solar system. Here the emphasis is not just on details but on the

Table 3.1 Goals at Multiple Levels of Difficulty for a Science Class

Level of Difficulty	Learning Goal	Task
Level 4 Knowledge Utilization: Investigating	The student will be able to investigate the gradual growth of knowledge about the solar system.	Select one of the current discoveries about the solar system we have studied in class. Investigate how the discovery came about and how it changed our thinking about the solar system.
Level 3 Analysis: Matching	The student will be able to identify similarities and differences between various planets in the solar system.	Identify two planets in our solar system, and compare them on two or more characteristics of your choice.
Level 2 Comprehension: Integrating	The student will be able to explain the critical features of the Copernican model of the solar system.	Explain what you consider to be the most important features of the Copernican model of the solar system.
Level 1 Retrieval: Recognizing and Recalling	The student will be able to recognize or recall important details about the solar system.	Briefly explain the following terms: • Planetary rings • Light year • Astronomical unit Determine if the following statements are true or false: 1. The path of objects traveling around the sun follows a law of planetary motion discovered by German astronomer Johannes Kepler in the early 1600s. 2. There are seventy-three known moons in the solar system. 3. Jupiter is a dwarf planet. 4. The term *celestial object* does not include earth. 5. Mercury has fifteen planetary rings. 6. The moon is about one-third the size of earth. 7. Venus is the coldest planet in the solar system. 8. Astronomers often measure distances within the solar system in astronomical units.

Source: *Designing and Assessing Educational Objectives* (Marzano & Kendall, 2008, p. 168) Reprinted with permission.

distinction between the critical versus noncritical information about the solar system. The third level requires students to go beyond factual knowledge regarding the solar system and generate information that is not immediately obvious—in this case, that information involves similarities and differences between two specific planets. The objective at the fourth level goes beyond knowledge of the solar system per se. It requires students to trace the development of information about the solar system.

The four levels of learning goals depicted in table 3.1 represent a progression from fairly simple to fairly complex. As we will discuss in subsequent chapters, such a progression provides teachers with many powerful options both in terms of instruction and assessment. Specifically, in chapter 4, we will consider in depth how to organize learning into a rubric or scale that allows students to see their progress over time regarding a given topic. An abbreviated form of that scale is shown in table 3.2.

Table 3.2 Abbreviated Scale Involving Learning Goals at Different Levels of Difficulty

Score 4.0	More complex learning goal
Score 3.0	Target learning goal
Score 2.0	Simpler learning goal
Score 1.0	With help, partial success at score 2.0 content and score 3.0 content
Score 0.0	Even with help, no success

We consider a more detailed form of this scale in chapter 4 (table 4.2, page 67). Briefly though, the scale depicted in table 3.2 requires three learning goals. The target learning goal is the goal initially designed by the teacher for the whole class. It is placed in score 3.0 position on the scale. A more complex goal is placed in the score 4.0 position, and a simpler goal is placed in the score 2.0 position. Score 1.0 and score 0.0 don't require new goals; they involve students' successful performance (or lack of performance) *with help*.

To effectively use the scale, it is necessary to write goals at different levels of complexity. This is where the New Taxonomy can be of value. As table 3.1 shows, it involves four levels of complexity:

- Level 4—Knowledge Utilization
- Level 3—Analysis
- Level 2—Comprehension
- Level 1—Retrieval

Retrieval goals require the recognition and recall of basic information and the execution of procedures. The level 1 learning goal in table 3.1 requires students to retrieve knowledge; they must recognize or recall basic details about the solar system.

Comprehension goals involve identifying the critical features of knowledge. At this level, students must be able to articulate and represent the major ideas and supporting details regarding knowledge. The level 2 learning goal in table 3.1 requires students to explain the critical features of the solar system.

Analysis goals involve reasoned extensions of knowledge. They are sometimes referred to as "higher order" because they require students to make inferences that go beyond what was directly taught. The level 3 goal in table 3.1 requires students to identify similarities and differences between two related planets. This information would not be obvious when studying planets in isolation; students would more likely have to infer similarities and differences between planets.

Knowledge utilization goals require students to use new knowledge in the context of a robust task. Robust tasks are the venue in which individuals use knowledge to address real-world issues. The level 4 goal in table 3.1 requires students to engage in a real-world task: investigating the development of knowledge regarding the solar system.

Each of the four levels of the New Taxonomy involves specific mental processes. This is depicted in table 3.3.

Table 3.3 Mental Processes Associated With Each Level of the New Taxonomy

Level of Difficulty	Mental Processes
Level 4: Knowledge Utilization	Decision Making
	Problem Solving
	Experimenting
	Investigating
Level 3: Analysis	Matching
	Classifying
	Analyzing Errors
	Generalizing
	Specifying
Level 2: Comprehension	Integrating
	Symbolizing
Level 1: Retrieval	Recognizing
	Recalling
	Executing

In the remainder of this chapter, we consider the four levels of the New Taxonomy and the mental processes associated with each level.

Level 1: Retrieval

The process of retrieval can vary somewhat depending on the type of knowledge involved and the degree of processing required. To understand these differences, it is important to keep in mind the distinction between declarative knowledge (information) and procedural knowledge (skills, strategies, and processes). Retrieval of information is either a matter of *recognizing* or *recalling*. Recognizing can be described as determining whether information is accurate or inaccurate. Recalling, by contrast, requires students to produce information from permanent memory. For example, a goal that requires students to select a synonym from among a set of words relies upon recognition. A synonym is provided for the student, and the student must recognize it. A goal that requires students to produce a synonym employs recall. In addition to recognizing the term *synonym*, the student must produce an appropriate example. This distinction constitutes a hierarchy of difficulty in itself: recalling is a more complex mental process than recognizing.

Although information (declarative knowledge) is only recognized or recalled, skills, strategies, and processes (procedural knowledge) can be *executed* as well. Execution means that a series of steps is carried out, something occurs, and a product results. For example, consider the procedure for multicolumn subtraction: a quantity is computed when the steps are carried out. Thus, we say that procedural knowledge is executed, whereas information is recognized and recalled. However, it is also true that procedural knowledge can be recognized and recalled because all procedures contain embedded information. For example, to perform multicolumn subtraction (procedural knowledge), students must know information about place value (declarative knowledge). Consequently, they could be asked to recall or recognize this information in addition to executing the steps of multicolumn subtraction.

Recognizing Goals and Tasks

Recognizing goals and tasks for declarative knowledge and procedural knowledge are depicted in table 3.4.

Table 3.4 Recognizing Goals and Tasks

Type of Knowledge	General Statement of Knowledge	Goal Statement	Sample Task
Declarative Knowledge (Information)	Information about paragraphs	Students will be able to recognize accurate statements about or examples of properly constructed paragraphs.	Which of the following statements about the construction of paragraphs is true (more than one may be true): A. Each paragraph has one sentence. B. Each paragraph begins with an indentation. C. Paragraphs are designed to organize and complete thoughts. D. Paragraphs are designed to conclude essays.
	Information about the presidents of the United States	Students will be able to recognize accurate statements about the first president and current president of the United States.	Identify each of the following statements as true about our first president, our current president, or neither: A. He was originally elected as a vice president. B. He received 100% of the electoral votes. C. He was responsible for the Jay Treaty. D. He left a governorship in Texas for the office of the presidency.
	Information about statistics	Students will be able to select examples of descriptive statistics from a list.	Which of the following is an example of a descriptive statistic? A. Standard deviation B. Correlation C. Chi-square D. Regression coefficient

Continued on next page →

Type of Knowledge	General Statement of Knowledge	Goal Statement	Sample Task
Declarative Knowledge (Information)	Information about cells	Students will be able to recognize accurate statements about cellular respiration.	Use the given words to fill in the blanks in the following statement: Cellular respiration is the process of _____ food _____. A. Oxidizing: atoms B. Oxidizing: molecules C. Decaying: energies D. Separating: molecules
Procedural Knowledge (Mental and Psychomotor Skills, Strategies, and Processes)	The process of going through an obstacle course	Students will be able to identify the obstacles and the order of obstacles in an obstacle course.	Which of the following is the correct order of obstacles in the obstacle course? A. Rope climb, wall scale, limbo bar B. Wall scale, limbo bar, traffic cone run C. Limbo bar, traffic cone run, rope climb D. None of the above
	The process of reading a map	Students will be able to select from a list the steps required to locate a city on a map.	From the list of steps in front of you, fill in the blanks that correctly complete the following statement: The first step in locating a city on a map is _____, the second is _____, and the last is _____.
	The process of reducing complex fractions	Students will be able to identify the correct sequence of steps necessary for reducing complex fractions.	Which of the following lists the correct order of steps for reducing complex fractions? A. Finding a least common multiple, dividing both the numerator and denominator by the LCM, simplifying B. Finding the least common denominator in all fractions in the problem, multiplying both the numerator and denominator by the LCD, simplifying

Type of Knowledge	General Statement of Knowledge	Goal Statement	Sample Task
Procedural Knowledge (Mental and Psychomotor Skills, Strategies, and Processes)			C. Dividing all fractions in the numerator and the denominator, squaring the quotient, finding the greatest common multiple, multiplying both the numerator and denominator by the GCM, simplifying D. None of the above
	The process of performing a scientific experiment	Students will be able to recognize accurate examples of rigorously performed scientific experiments.	Read the following examples of scientific experiments performed step by step. Which of them was the most rigorous?

A general statement of knowledge appears in the second column of table 3.4. Recall from the discussion in chapter 2 that frequently teachers must work with very general statements when designing their learning goals. The learning goals derived from these general statements are depicted in the third column. Finally, the fourth column provides a sample task for each goal statement.

Again, it is worth noting that each learning goal in column three of table 3.4 begins with the phrase "Students will be able to." Recall that this contradicts the recommendation in chapter 2 that declarative goals use the format "Students will understand," and procedural goals have the format "Students will be able to." This is because once the distinction between declarative and procedural knowledge is well established, it is best to use specific verbs when designing learning goals for different levels of the New Taxonomy. The generic phrase "Students will be able to" allows the teacher to insert a variety of verbs that will accommodate any level of the New Taxonomy.

Verbs that teachers frequently use when designing recognizing goals and tasks include the following:

- Recognize (from a list)
- Select from (a list)
- Identify (from a list)
- Determine (if the following statements are true)

As shown in table 3.4, tasks for recognizing goals commonly require students to determine whether statements are true or false or to select true statements from a list.

Recalling Goals and Tasks

Recalling involves producing accurate information as opposed to simply recognizing it. Table 3.5 (page 32) provides sample recalling goals and tasks for declarative knowledge and procedural knowledge.

Table 3.5 Recalling Goals and Tasks

Type of Knowledge	General Statement of Knowledge	Goal Statement	Sample Task
Declarative Knowledge (Information)	Information about software programs	Students will be able to explain the purposes and advantages of Microsoft Word.	Explain why Microsoft Word was created and what it does that is unique.
	Information about color	Students will be able to name primary and secondary colors.	Make two lists, one that includes the names of the primary colors and one that includes the names of the secondary colors.
	Information about percentages	Students will be able to describe a percentage in terms of a ratio.	What does 50% mean in terms of a ratio?
	Information about atoms	Students will be able to list the major subatomic particles.	Create a list including the names of all the subatomic particles we have studied.
Procedural Knowledge (Mental and Psychomotor Skills, Strategies, and Processes)	The process of addition	Students will be able to list the steps involved in the process of two-digit to two-digit addition.	On the board is a two-digit number that has been added to a two-digit number to find a sum. Explain the basic process of adding these numbers.
	The process of making scientific predictions	Students will be able to describe how to make a reasonable prediction regarding the outcome of a scientific experiment.	Describe the steps involved in making a prediction regarding an experiment.
	The process of creating original documents using computer software	Students will be able to describe the steps and options involved in creating a PowerPoint presentation.	Explain the steps you should follow and the choices you will make when creating a PowerPoint presentation.
	The process of performing music	Students will be able to list the steps involved in warming up to play a specific piece of music on the piano.	Using the composition provided, give a brief written description of the steps you would go through to "warm up" before performing this composition on the piano.

Verbs that teachers frequently use when designing recalling goals and tasks include the following:

- Exemplify
- Name
- List
- Label
- State

- Describe

- Identify who

- Describe what

- Identify where

- Identify when

As shown in the last column of table 3.5, tasks for recalling goals are usually in the form of short constructed-response items. Students must name something or provide a list of things.

Executing Goals and Tasks

Executing involves actually carrying out a mental or psychomotor procedure as opposed to simply recognizing or recalling information about procedures. Again, consider multicolumn subtraction. A teacher could write a recognizing goal for this procedure that requires students to identify accurate statements about multicolumn subtraction. She could write a recalling goal that requires students to describe how to perform multicolumn subtraction. Neither of those goals actually requires students to perform multicolumn subtraction, however. This is the domain of execution—asking students to demonstrate a skill, strategy, or process.

There is a great deal of misunderstanding regarding executing goals, particularly as they relate to complex mental and psychomotor procedures. Although it is true that executing is at the lowest level of the New Taxonomy (because it is a form of retrieval), it can be the highest level of expectation for students when a complex mental or psychomotor procedure is involved. Consider the mental process of writing a persuasive essay. The actual execution of this process is a complex feat indeed, requiring the management of many interacting components. The same can be said for the process of playing basketball, a psychomotor procedure. How then, could a teacher ever expect to construct goals beyond the retrieval level for complex procedures? The answer is that executing, in fact, might be the highest level of expectation for students for complex procedures. Stated differently, a teacher might not have goals above the executing level for complex procedures such as writing a persuasive essay and playing basketball. This does not mean, however, that goals at different levels of complexity cannot be designed for complex procedures.

One way to differentiate levels of complexity for complex procedures is to break them into smaller component parts. For some students, a teacher might focus on one or two elements only for a complex procedure. For example, for students less skilled at writing persuasive essays the emphasis might be on stating a clear claim with some sentences supporting the claim. With this more narrow focus for less skilled students, goals for more skilled students would incorporate more components of the overall complex procedure. For example, a learning goal for the complex procedure of writing a persuasive essay might include a clear claim and specific evidence for the claim presented in a coherent manner. For students more familiar with writing persuasive essays, the goal might also specify that each piece of evidence should be backed up with information supporting its validity.

Like writing a persuasive essay, playing basketball includes a variety of embedded procedures. For less skilled students, the emphasis might be on dribbling only. The goal for more skilled students might include dribbling while running down the court and passing to the other players. Again, as levels of difficulty increase, the procedure involves more components acting in tandem. Robert Marzano and Mark Haystead (2008) have outlined how this spiraling effect for curriculum can be accomplished in the areas of language arts, mathematics, science, and social studies.

Executing goals and tasks are depicted in table 3.6.

Table 3.6 Executing Goals and Tasks

Type of Knowledge	General Statement of Knowledge	Goal Statement	Sample Task
Declarative Knowledge (Information)	N/A	N/A	N/A
Procedural Knowledge (Mental and Psychomotor Skills, Strategies, and Processes)	The skill of kicking a ball	Students will be able to use their feet to stop and kick a ball.	When it is your turn, I will kick the ball to you. Using only your feet, stop the ball and kick it back to me.
	The process of singing with a group	Students will be able to use correct tempo when singing with a group.	In your small groups, you will come up to the piano and sing the song you have learned. When you are singing, pay particular attention to the song's tempo.
	The process of producing an original photograph	Students will be able to create an original photograph with particular attention to light, scale, and definition.	The school's greenhouse is an ideal place for taking photos that focus on creative uses of light, scale, and definition. When you are taking your photos, pay special attention to these elements.
	The process of writing a short story	Students will be able to write a short story that uses deliberate shifts in perspective.	We have read a few short stories that use shifts in perspective. Take the story you wrote during our last unit that has one perspective, and rewrite it to include one or more shifts in perspective.

Verbs that teachers frequently use when designing executing goals and tasks include the following:

- Use
- Demonstrate
- Show
- Make
- Complete
- Draft

A common format for executing tasks is short constructed-response items. When a physical procedure is being addressed, the task will include a demonstration. For example, if a learning goal in a physical education class involves the overhand throw of a baseball, the task would be to physically demonstrate the procedure. In the case of a mental procedure, tasks might include forced choice–type items such as multiple choice. For example, if a learning goal dealt with multicolumn multiplication, items such as the following might be used to determine whether students have attained the learning goal.

Which of the following is the correct answer for this multiplication problem: 341 × 4782?

730,662

1,730,662

1,630,662

630,662

In summary, there are three types of retrieval goals and tasks that can be designed: recognizing goals, recalling goals, and executing goals. Exercise 3.1 provides practice in identifying the three types of retrieval goals. (See page 58 for a reproducible of this exercise and page 106 for a reproducible answer sheet. Visit **marzanoresearch.com/classroomstrategies** to download all the exercises and answers in this book.)

Exercise 3.1
Identifying Different Types of Retrieval Goals

Following are some examples of goal statements at the retrieval level. For each, identify whether it is more closely a recognizing, recalling, or executing goal statement. Keep in mind that there is some fluidity and overlap between and among the types of retrieval goals.

1. Students will be able to identify from a list the steps involved in photosynthesis.

    Recognizing   Recalling   Executing

2. Students will be able to play a piece of music.

    Recognizing   Recalling   Executing

3. Students will be able to name six prominent world political leaders.

    Recognizing   Recalling   Executing

4. Students will be able to list the continents.

    Recognizing   Recalling   Executing

5. Students will be able to identify accurate vs. inaccurate information about presidential candidates.

    Recognizing   Recalling   Executing

6. Students will be able to list the major combatant nations of World War II.

    Recognizing   Recalling   Executing

7. Students will be able to select mammals from a list of animals.

    Recognizing   Recalling   Executing

8. Students will be able to identify examples of complete sentences.

    Recognizing   Recalling   Executing

9. Students will be able to list examples of proper nouns.

    Recognizing   Recalling   Executing

10. Students will be able to perform addition using two-digit numbers.

    Recognizing   Recalling   Executing

Level 2: Comprehension

Comprehension goals require students to demonstrate an understanding of the overall structure of knowledge—the critical versus noncritical aspects of the knowledge. There are two related types of comprehension goals a teacher might design: integrating goals and symbolizing goals.

Integrating Goals and Tasks

Integrating involves distilling knowledge down to its key characteristics and organizing it into a parsimonious, generalized form. Integrating goals and tasks require students to describe the critical (as opposed to noncritical) information regarding content. Examples of integrating goals and tasks are provided in table 3.7.

Verbs that teachers frequently use when designing integrating goals and tasks include the following:

- Describe how or why
- Describe the key parts of
- Describe the effects
- Describe the relationship between
- Explain ways in which
- Paraphrase
- Summarize

As the samples in table 3.7 illustrate, tasks for integrating goals are usually short constructed response in nature as they require students to describe or explain something. It is important to note that integrating goals for procedural knowledge are typically not addressed until students can actually perform the procedure. For example, consider the integrating goal in table 3.7: students are expected to summarize the essential elements of proofreading and describe their functions. It would make little sense to ask students to do this while they are struggling with the steps or the strategies included in the procedure. However, once students get to a point where they can perform the process independently, asking them to discern the essential elements of the process can provide information that will help them fine-tune the process.

Symbolizing Goals and Tasks

Symbolizing goals require students to translate their understanding into some pictorial, graphic, or pictographic representation. Another way of saying this is that symbolizing goals require students to translate what they have produced from an integrating goal into some nonlinguistic form. Consequently, symbolizing goals can be and are frequently used in tandem with integrating goals. Sample symbolizing goals and tasks are presented in table 3.8 (page 38).

Verbs that teachers frequently use when constructing symbolizing goals and tasks include the following:

- Symbolize
- Depict
- Represent
- Illustrate

Table 3.7 Integrating Goals and Tasks

Type of Knowledge	General Statement of Knowledge	Goal Statement	Sample Task
Declarative Knowledge (Information)	Information about the earth's rotation and orbit	Students will be able to explain the relationship between the rotation and orbit of the earth and the changing of days and seasons.	Explain how our days and seasons change respective of the rotation and orbit of the earth.
	Information about Harriet Tubman	Students will be able to make clear why Harriet Tubman is known for her contributions to the Underground Railroad.	Explain the purpose and major achievements of the Underground Railroad in terms of Harriet Tubman's contributions.
	Information about the relationship between circles and spheres	Students will be able to explain how the area of a circle determines the volume of a corresponding sphere.	Using the formula and the calculations provided to you, explain the relationship between the area of a circle and the volume of its corresponding sphere.
	Information about archetypal theme	Students will be able to discuss themes common to multiple texts and make connections between theme and archetype.	Consider the last three books we read. What do they have in common thematically, and how do those themes speak to the archetypes we have discussed?
Procedural Knowledge (Mental and Psychomotor Skills, Strategies, and Processes)	The process of proofreading	Students will be able to summarize the essential elements of proofreading and describe their functions.	Look at the passage provided. How would you proofread it and in what order? Explain why the order of steps is important.
	The process of creating a simple circuit	Students will be able to describe the steps involved in creating a simple circuit.	Given the following materials, describe the steps you would take to create a simple circuit. Why is the order of steps important?
	The process of choosing appropriate research sources and information	Students will be able to describe the steps they took in choosing the research sources and information used in a persuasive essay.	We will be having some informal teacher/student conferences during the next few days in which we will discuss your recent essays. Please come prepared to talk about how you chose the resources you used and explain why each step you followed was important.
	The process of using the order of operations to solve algebra problems	Students will be able to summarize how to apply the order of operations to solve a problem.	We have solved a few equations using the order of operations. Summarize the process, and then solve an equation on your own using your summary as a guide.

- Draw
- Show
- Use models
- Diagram
- Chart

Table 3.8 Symbolizing Goals and Tasks

Type of Knowledge	General Statement of Knowledge	Goal Statement	Sample Task
Declarative Knowledge (Information)	Information about the solar system	Students will be able to create a model that shows the locations of the planets in our solar system.	Using the materials provided, create a model of the solar system. Be sure to use appropriately sized objects to represent the planets.
	Information about percentages	Students will be able to draw a pie chart representing various percentages of a whole.	Create a pie chart that represents the following statement: Bill has 45% of the lottery tickets, Sherry has 15%, and Merle has 40%.
	Information about a free-market economy	Students will be able to draw a flowchart depicting the elements of a free-market economy and how they work together.	After considering the most important elements of a free-market economy, create a flowchart that depicts these elements and how they work together.
	Information about measures of central tendency	Students will be able to represent the mean, median, and mode of a given set of data.	Create a skit representing the mean, median, and mode of the following set of data.
Procedural Knowledge (Mental and Psychomotor Skills, Strategies, and Processes)	The skill of throwing a ball overhand	Students will be able to illustrate the steps in throwing a ball overhand and explain the importance of each step.	Create a flipbook for the process of throwing a ball overhand. For each page, include a caption about the importance of each step.
	The process of collecting simple data	Students will be able to create a flowchart that represents the steps involved in simple data collection.	Create a flowchart that represents the process you went through when conducting our schoolwide surveys.
	The skill of executing a turn while skiing	Students will be able to present images that illustrate a correct ski turn.	On your computers are avatars wearing skis. Using your controls, demonstrate a proper ski turn.
	The process of creating a composition that focuses on expressing an emotion	Students will be able to graphically organize one or more combinations of techniques that can be used in painting to convey emotion.	After thinking about which of the painting techniques we have studied express emotion the best, create a canvas that depicts a plan for painting.

As evidenced in table 3.8, tasks for symbolizing goals require students to produce and explain a pictorial, graphic, or pictographic representation of content.

In summary, there are two types of comprehension goals: integrating and symbolizing goals. Exercise 3.2 provides some practice in identifying each of them. (See page 59 for a reproducible of this exercise and page 108 for a reproducible answer sheet. Visit **marzanoresearch.com/classroomstrategies** to download all the exercises and answers in this book.)

Exercise 3.2
Identifying Different Types of Comprehension Goals

Following are some examples of goal statements at the comprehension level. For each, identify whether it is more closely an integrating or symbolizing goal statement. Keep in mind that there is some fluidity and overlap between and among the comprehension goals.

1. Students will be able to describe the major components of an organism's behavior cycle.

    Integrating   Symbolizing

2. Students will be able to create a flowchart that shows the steps involved in tying a shoe.

    Integrating   Symbolizing

3. Students will be able to describe the key reasons eating healthy food provides the body with more energy.

    Integrating   Symbolizing

4. Students will be able to describe the major contributions to society made by Dr. Martin Luther King, Jr.

    Integrating   Symbolizing

5. Students will be able to summarize the results of a scientific experiment.

    Integrating   Symbolizing

6. Students will be able to diagram the transitions between key ideas in an expository text.

    Integrating   Symbolizing

7. Students will be able to create pictorial representations of the cause-and-effect sequence of an event in history.

    Integrating   Symbolizing

8. Students will be able to paraphrase the important points made by a speaker.

    Integrating   Symbolizing

9. Students will be able to use manipulatives to demonstrate the process of multiplication.

    Integrating   Symbolizing

10. Students will be able to describe the defining aspects of a musical genre.

    Integrating   Symbolizing

Level 3: Analysis

Analysis goals require students to go beyond what was actually taught in class and make inferences that create new awareness. There are five types of analysis goals a teacher might design: matching goals, classifying goals, analyzing errors goals, generalizing goals, and specifying goals.

Matching Goals and Tasks

Matching involves identifying similarities and differences. Table 3.9 (page 40) presents matching goals and tasks for declarative and procedural knowledge.

Table 3.9 Matching Goals and Tasks

Type of Knowledge	General Statement of Knowledge	Goal Statement	Sample Task
Declarative Knowledge (Information)	Information about prime numbers	Students will be able to distinguish between prime and nonprime numbers.	Organize the following numbers into two categories: prime numbers and nonprime numbers. Then explain what is common to all prime numbers. 3, 4, 8, 9, 0, 16, 15
	Information about literary genres	Students will be able to discriminate between fiction and nonfiction texts.	Explain the differences between fiction and nonfiction books.
	Information about the relationships between climate change and human habitat	Students will be able to create analogies regarding the relationship between climate change and human habitat.	Think about the relationship between the earth's climate change and human habit. What other two things share the same relationship? Explain.
	Information about infectious diseases	Students will be able to categorize diseases according to their similarities.	Organize the given list of diseases into two or more categories. Explain your criteria for inclusion in each category.
Procedural Knowledge (Mental and Psychomotor Skills, Strategies, and Processes)	The process of finding information in a text	Students will be able to determine processes similar to that of finding information in a text.	Describe a process similar to that of finding information in a text. Explain why they are similar.
	The processes of subtracting and dividing whole numbers	Students will be able to describe how subtracting and dividing are alike and how they differ.	Describe how subtracting and dividing are similar and how they are different.
	The processes of making direct measurements and making estimations	Students will be able to compare the processes of making direct measurements and making estimations.	Using specific examples, describe the similarities and differences between how you would make a direct measurement and how you would make an estimation.
	The process of performing specific types of dances	Students will be able to compare two types of dances.	Select and compare two specific types of dance we have been studying, such as jazz and hip hop. Focus on how the dance steps and movements are similar and different.

Verbs that teachers frequently use when designing matching goals and tasks include the following:

- Categorize

- Compare and contrast

- Differentiate

- Discriminate

- Distinguish

- Sort

- Create an analogy

- Create a metaphor

It is important to note that matching can involve more than two examples of a specific type of knowledge. For example, as described by Marzano and Kendall (2008), a student demonstrates the ability to match by organizing historically important wars into two or more groups based on their similarities. Consequently, the following would be an example of a task that could be used to assess a matching goal:

> We have been studying a number of wars that were important historically for one reason or another. Organize these wars into two or more groups and explain how the wars within each group are similar. Also explain how the wars are different from group to group:
>
> - The French Revolution
>
> - The American Revolution
>
> - The Hundred Years' War
>
> - The Vietnam War
>
> - The French and Indian War
>
> - The Spanish-American War
>
> - World War I
>
> - World War II
>
> - Desert Storm
>
> - The War in Afghanistan

Matching can also employ an analogy format like the following:

> Explain how the relationship between a bone and a skeleton is similar to and different from the relationship between a word and a sentence.

Analogy formats require students to identify how a relationship between one pair of elements is similar to the relationship between a second pair of elements—in this case, how the relationship between a bone and a skeleton is similar to the relationship between a word and a sentence.

Finally, matching tasks can also employ a metaphor format like the following:

> Explain the following metaphor: Helen Keller was the Frederick Douglass of her family.

To complete this task, a student must determine how Helen Keller and Frederick Douglass are alike at an abstract level because they bear little resemblance at a concrete level. This is the essence of a metaphor—identifying abstract similarities when there are few or no concrete similarities. Tasks for matching goals are most commonly short constructed response in nature.

Classifying Goals and Tasks

The mental process of classifying goes beyond organizing items into groups or categories. As described previously, such activity is better thought of as matching. Instead, classifying involves identifying the superordinate category in which knowledge belongs as well as the subordinate categories (if any) for knowledge. To illustrate, a goal that requires students to organize the fifty states into three categories based on voting tendencies in presidential elections (Democratic, Republican, or Independent) would be considered a classifying task because it requires students to identify superordinate categories to which each state belongs. Conversely, a learning goal that asks students to organize the fifty states into categories of their own choosing would be considered a matching goal because it requires students to organize by similarities and differences of their own design. Table 3.10 presents examples of classifying goals and tasks for declarative and procedural knowledge.

Verbs that teachers frequently use when designing classifying goals and tasks include the following:

- Classify
- Organize
- Sort
- Identify a broader category
- Identify categories
- Identify different types

Most commonly, assessment tasks for classifying goals are short constructed response in nature.

Analyzing Errors Goals and Tasks

Goals that involve analyzing errors require students to identify factual or logical errors in knowledge or processing errors in the execution of procedural knowledge. Table 3.11 (page 44) depicts goals and tasks for analyzing errors in declarative and procedural knowledge.

Verbs that teachers frequently use when designing learning goals and tasks that involve analyzing errors include the following:

- Identify errors
- Identify problems
- Identify issues
- Identify misunderstandings
- Assess
- Critique
- Diagnose
- Evaluate
- Edit
- Revise

Table 3.10 Classifying Goals and Tasks

Type of Knowledge	General Statement of Knowledge	Goal Statement	Sample Task
Declarative Knowledge (Information)	Information about geometric shapes	Students will be able to organize a set of shapes according to their class of geometric properties.	From the objects in front of you, pick out the triangles, and explain what makes a triangle unique.
	Information about human internal organs	Students will be able to categorize types of human organs according to their functions.	Which of the human organs are meant to clean our bodies? Explain each of your choices.
	Information about organic and inorganic chemistry	Students will be able to classify compounds into organic and inorganic categories.	In front of you is a list of chemical compounds, some of which are compounds containing C-H bonds. Classify each as organic or inorganic, and explain your answer.
	Information about the periodic table of elements	Students will be able to sort elements in the periodic table according to a specific trait such as rarity or combustibility.	Using the periodic table as a guide, make a list of elements that all share the quality of being metallic.
Procedural Knowledge (Mental and Psychomotor Skills, Strategies, and Processes)	The process of correcting errors in spelling	Students will be able to classify spell-checking as among the proofreading and editing skills needed to prepare a written work for publishing.	Correcting for spelling is a task that is part of what collection of important skills? What other skills are commonly used at the same time?
	The process of ensuring personal safety	Students will be able to identify certain rules as those that are established and followed for personal safety.	We have been learning what to do in the event of a fire or a tornado. What kinds of rules are these examples of? What other rules are there like this?
	The process of cardiovascular exercise	Students will be able to identify categories of exercise according to their effects on the human cardiovascular system.	Phil wants an exercise program that reduces his stress level and increases his muscular strength. He does not need to burn many calories. Which exercise regimen would you recommend and why?
	The process of using specific types of tools to collect data	Students will be able to classify tools and equipment as those used in gathering data.	When using microscopes and graduated cylinders, what types of skills are we engaged in? What are other examples of this type of skill?

Table 3.11 Analyzing Errors Goals

Type of Knowledge	General Statement of Knowledge	Goal Statement	Sample Task
Declarative Knowledge (Information)	Information about stereotyping	Students will be able to identify problems with stereotypes.	Think of stereotypes that might be applied to you or to someone you know well. Explain what is inaccurate about these stereotypes.
	Information about grammar	Students will be able to identify grammar errors in a text.	Read the 10 sentences in front of you. Explain the grammatical errors made in each sentence.
	Information about the use of nuclear energy	Students will identify common misconceptions about use of nuclear waste.	Read the passage provided you. What are some errors in the author's understanding of nuclear waste?
	Details about current political issues	Students will be able to determine the accuracy of the content presented in a presidential debate.	Review the information delivered by each candidate in last night's debate to determine whether a candidate has simplified an issue in ways that could mislead anyone who is not familiar with the details.
Procedural Knowledge (Mental and Psychomotor Skills, Strategies, and Processes)	The skill of importing a table from a spreadsheet to a Word file	Students will be able to diagnose errors in data formatting based on an understanding of the steps used to import data.	You've imported a table from a spreadsheet document into the paper you are writing, but the table loses some formatting and overruns the page margins. What is the likely cause of this error?
	The process of playing a team sport	Students will be able to diagnose specific problems they have with teamwork in a specific sport.	Now that we have finished our game, sit down and evaluate your own performance in terms of teamwork. What problems do you have with things like passing the ball, encouraging teammates, and blocking for a member of your team?
	The process of performing a specific skill of the student's choice	Students will be able to identify sport performance errors based on an understanding of sport-specific skills.	Videotape your execution of a skill that you want to improve. Review the tape in slow motion to identify any incorrect body positions.
	Approaches to solving specific problems	Students will be able to evaluate errors made when solving a specific type of mathematical problem.	In front of you are a mathematical problem and three different approaches taken by different students to solve it. What error did each student make?

Assessment items and tasks for analyzing errors goals are commonly short constructed response in nature. In addition, more structured formats can be used. For example, consider the following tasks:

> Marty is older than Louis. He eats more fats than Louis does and less fiber. If it takes longer for Marty to digest food than it takes Louis, which of the following offers a correct explanation as to why? What errors were made in the other explanations?
>
> Explanation 1: Marty's digestive process is slower because he is old, and all of our body systems slow with age.
>
> Explanation 2: Because Marty eats more fats, he is heavier than Louis, and the heavier a person is the slower his digestion.
>
> Explanation 3: Because Marty is older than Louis, his metabolism is likely slower than Louis'. A slower metabolism combined with a higher fat and lower fiber intake (fat takes longer to digest than fiber) explains the difference.
>
> Explanation 4: Louis' body takes longer to digest food because he eats more fiber, and fiber takes longer than any other food to digest. His age in comparison with Marty's makes no difference.
>
> Explanation 5: The variances in digestion times are strictly genetic. Marty's body processes food more slowly because of his genetics, not because of his age or his high-fat, low-fiber intake.

The preceding example involves declarative knowledge (information). The following example focuses on the mental procedure of finding the mean of a set of data:

> Bess is finding the mean of a set of data given to her by the teacher. If she does the following, explain what she will have done wrong:
>
> 1. Organizes the numbers in the data set from least to greatest
>
> 2. Counts the number of times each number appears in the data set
>
> 3. Identifies the number that appears most often in the data set as the mean

Generalizing Goals and Tasks

Generalizing goals require students to infer new generalizations and principles from information that is known or stated. Generalizing goals involve inductive thinking on the part of students in that they must create general statements based on specific pieces of information. Table 3.12 (page 46) depicts generalizing goals and tasks for declarative and procedural knowledge.

Verbs that teachers frequently use when designing generalizing goals and tasks include the following:

- Generalize

- What conclusions can be drawn

- What inferences can be made

- Create a generalization

Table 3.12 Generalizing Goals and Tasks

Type of Knowledge	General Statement of Knowledge	Goal Statement	Sample Task
Declarative Knowledge (Information)	Information about the results of a basic experiment	Students will make and defend conclusions drawn from a set of results.	Based on the result of our experiment with static electricity, what would you say causes it? Explain your answer.
	Information about classroom rules	Students will develop and be able to explain their conclusions about the consequences of breaking classroom rules.	What do you think the purpose of classroom rules is? What should happen to students who break the rules? Based on the school year so far, do you think the teacher and other students agree? Explain your answer.
	Information about proper diet	Given a set of details about proper diet, students will be able to create generalizations about designing healthy meals.	You have been presented with information about proper diet. What conclusions can you draw about how to design meals for a day?
	Information about Chinese government	Students will be able to trace the development of Chinese government from 1800–2000 and make a generalization about whether or not the governing has benefitted the people.	Many different groups or individuals have been in power in China over the last 200 years. Consider the living conditions in China in 1800 and the living conditions in China today. In general, do you think those in control have done a good job? Why or why not?
Procedural Knowledge (Mental and Psychomotor Skills, Strategies, and Processes)	The process of increasing physical flexibility	Students will be able to create and justify a set of exercises designed to maintain flexibility.	Based on what we have been studying about aging, design an exercise program that will keep you as flexible as possible. Explain why your program should work.
	The process of creating a basic pattern	Given a basic pattern, students will be able to create and defend a rule that would apply to its extension.	The colors in front of you create a pattern. What do you think determines the rule for this pattern? What color will come next? Why?
	The process of sewing a garment	Students will be able to create a rule regarding the most and least effective stitch types.	After having used each of the stitch types presented in class with delicate and tough cloths, which stitch type would you say is the most universally effective, and why?
	The process of using nonverbal language specific to people who speak a specific language	Students will be able to generalize about common gestures and their meanings to native speakers of a specific language.	What can be said generally about the motions and gestures common to native French speakers? Explain what led you to your conclusions.

- Create a principle

- Create a rule

- Trace the development of

- Form conclusions

Assessment items and tasks for generalizing goals commonly employ short constructed-response formats.

Specifying Goals and Tasks

Specifying goals require students to make and defend predictions about what might happen or what will necessarily happen in a given situation. Specifying goals are deductive in nature in that they require students to reason from a rule or a principle to make and defend predictions. Table 3.13 depicts specifying goals and tasks for declarative and procedural knowledge.

Verbs that teachers frequently use when designing specifying goals and tasks include the following:

- Make and defend

- Predict

Table 3.13 Specifying Goals and Tasks

Type of Knowledge	General Statement of Knowledge	Goal Statement	Sample Task
Declarative Knowledge (Information)	Information about the musical chords	Students will be able to predict which chords will go well together in a musical composition.	Now that you know chords, explain which chords will always go well together in a musical composition. Explain why.
	Information about using spices in cooking	Students will be able to judge what spices would best enhance a given dish.	If you are preparing a dish with Spanish influences, what spices would you know you should not use? Why?
	Information about environmental conditions and their effects on humankind	Students will be able to specify the prime environmental conditions for human survival.	After studying several climates and the health of humans living in them, make an ideal climate for people to live in. Describe the principles you used in creating your ideal climate.
	Information about conditional probability	Students will be able to speculate on the likelihood of one event given another.	If Don opened an Indian restaurant in a small, rural town and it failed, what do you think will happen to Jim's Ethiopian restaurant? What general principles did you follow to form your conclusions?

Continued on next page →

Type of Knowledge	General Statement of Knowledge	Goal Statement	Sample Task
Procedural Knowledge (Mental and Psychomotor Skills, Strategies, and Processes)	The process of playing volleyball	Students will be able to make and defend an inference on the likely strategy of an opponent if the opponent is presented with consistent behavior.	If you consistently rush the net after every serve, what would your opponent likely do in response? Explain what led you to your conclusions.
	The skill of measuring length, perimeter, and area	Students will be able to make and defend inferences about the results of measurements based on an understanding of the relationship between perimeter and area.	If you change the dimensions of a square so that it becomes a rectangle with the same unit area, how will its perimeter change? Explain how you know your answer is correct.
	The mental process of conducting an experiment	Students will be able to make and defend an inference about different types of experimental designs.	If you followed exactly the same steps for two experiments, but in one you used random assignment and in the other you did not, what are some things you could say about the results from the random study that you could not say about the other study? Explain.
	The process of writing a persuasive essay	Students will be able to make and defend an inference about the development of a persuasive essay.	Based on what you know about writing a persuasive essay, what are some things you know a beginning writer has to watch out for? Explain the rules or principles you used to construct your answer.

- Judge

- Deduce

- What would have to happen

- Develop an argument for

- Under what conditions

Assessment items and tasks for specifying goals commonly involve short constructed-response formats.

In summary, there are five types of analysis goals: matching goals, classifying goals, analyzing errors goals, generalizing goals, and specifying goals. Exercise 3.3 provides practice in identifying the various types of analysis goals. (See page 60 for a reproducible of this exercise and page 110 for a reproducible answer sheet. Visit **marzanoresearch.com/classroomstrategies** to download all the exercises and answers in this book.)

Exercise 3.3
Identifying Different Types of Analysis Goals

Following are some examples of goal statements at the analysis level. For each, identify whether it is more closely a matching, classifying, analyzing errors, generalizing, or specifying goal statement. Keep in mind that there is some fluidity and overlap between and among the types of analysis goals.

1. Students will be able to organize a group of sentences into the following categories: simple, compound, complex.

      Matching   Classifying   Analyzing Errors   Generalizing   Specifying

2. Given a group of statements, students will be able to generate conclusions that flow from them.

      Matching   Classifying   Analyzing Errors   Generalizing   Specifying

3. Students will be able to compare and contrast classical, romantic, and modern styles of music.

      Matching   Classifying   Analyzing Errors   Generalizing   Specifying

4. Students will be able to develop an office floor plan based on specific principles of communication and justify its layout.

      Matching   Classifying   Analyzing Errors   Generalizing   Specifying

5. Students will describe how their observations are similar or dissimilar to others' observations.

      Matching   Classifying   Analyzing Errors   Generalizing   Specifying

6. Students will be able to categorize types of statistical calculations according to their use.

      Matching   Classifying   Analyzing Errors   Generalizing   Specifying

7. Students will be able to identify and correct logical errors in a written argument.

      Matching   Classifying   Analyzing Errors   Generalizing   Specifying

8. Students will be able to infer the global implications of a proposed energy technology.

      Matching   Classifying   Analyzing Errors   Generalizing   Specifying

9. Students will be able to judge what colors would best enhance a workspace.

      Matching   Classifying   Analyzing Errors   Generalizing   Specifying

10. Students will be able to identify problems in the flow of their writing and correct them.

      Matching   Classifying   Analyzing Errors   Generalizing   Specifying

Level 4: Knowledge Utilization

Knowledge utilization goals require students to apply or use knowledge in specific situations. There are four types of knowledge utilization goals: decision-making goals, problem-solving goals, experimenting goals, and investigating goals. We consider each in this section.

Decision-Making Goals and Tasks

Decision-making goals require students to select among alternatives that initially appear equal. Table 3.14 (pages 50–51) depicts decision-making goals and tasks for declarative and procedural knowledge.

Verbs that teachers frequently use when designing decision-making goals and tasks include the following:

- Decide

- Select the best among the following alternatives

- Which among the following would be the best

- What is the best way

- Which of these is most suitable

Table 3.14 Decision-Making Goals and Tasks

Type of Knowledge	General Statement of Knowledge	Goal Statement	Sample Task
Declarative Knowledge (Information)	Information about healthy foods	Students will be able to decide which foods in a list are healthier than others.	All of the foods on the list you have been given have dairy in them. Which are the three healthiest choices? Explain your criteria.
	Information about safety procedures	Students will be able to determine which safety procedures are relevant to a given situation.	If you are approached by a stranger would you stop, drop, and roll or yell and run in the opposite direction? Why? What information did you use to make your decision?
	Information about the office of the American president	Students will be able to select the most effective peacetime leader from recent presidents.	Which of the last three presidents is the best peacetime leader? Explain your criteria.
	Information about research methods	When presented with a list of data collection techniques, students will be able to select the technique best suited to answering a specific research question.	If you want to know the standings of the presidential candidates among your peers, which data collection methods would you use and why? What criteria did you use to decide?
Procedural Knowledge (Mental and Psychomotor Skills, Strategies, and Processes)	Estimation skills and strategies	Students will be able to decide, based on a familiarity with estimation strategies, which strategies are appropriate for a particular problem type.	You were given three two-digit numbers—78, 92, and 65—and asked to quickly estimate the sum in your head. Identify at least two ways of doing this, and then explain which you would use in this case. Consider speed and accuracy in your decision.
	The process of determining the meaning of an unknown word	Students will be able to choose the best reference sources to determine the meaning of an unknown word.	Around the classroom are dictionaries, thesauruses, atlases, and almanacs. If you wanted to find the definition for a word, which one would you go to? Why?
	The process of learning new knowledge	Students will be able to decide, based on an understanding of learning strategies, the best way to learn new personally chosen content.	We have been studying ways to learn and remember new information. Four of these ways are (1) verbatim, (2) rehearsal, (3) mnemonic devices, and (4) extended practice. Select something you would like to learn, and decide which strategy would be best, given the content of your selection. Use at least two criteria when making your selection.

Type of Knowledge	General Statement of Knowledge	Goal Statement	Sample Task
	The process of creating a map	Students will be able to decide among a set of alternatives which type of map will work best for representing relevant information.	If you want to show the altering terrains and altitudes of a place, which map would be the best? Explain why.

Assessment tasks for decision-making goals typically require fairly extensive constructed-response formats.

Problem-Solving Goals and Tasks

Problem-solving goals require students to accomplish a goal for which obstacles or limiting conditions exist. Problem solving is closely related to decision making in that the latter is frequently a subcomponent of the former. However, whereas decision making does not involve obstacles to a goal, problem solving does. Table 3.15 depicts problem-solving goals and tasks for declarative and procedural knowledge.

Table 3.15 Problem-Solving Goals and Tasks

Type of Knowledge	General Statement of Knowledge	Goal Statement	Sample Task
Declarative Knowledge (Information)	Principles regarding ecosystems	Students will be able to address the major problems that threaten the survival of a given endangered species based on an understanding of requirements for food, temperature, and a supporting environment.	Based on what you have learned about an ecosystem, including the requirements for the survival of an endangered species who inhabits that ecosystem, develop a terrarium that you believe would give the selected species the best chance of survival. Identify the significant problems you faced in creating the right terrarium and how you solved them.
	Information about dimension in painting	Students will be able to describe ways to make a two-dimensional drawing appear three dimensional.	Describe how you would draw a three-dimensional image of a person on a two-dimensional page. What obstacles does this task present? How did you overcome them?
	Details about a specific alternative energy source	Students will be able to propose a solution for the adoption of a specific alternative energy source based on an understanding of the obstacles and trade-offs associated with its use.	We have been studying the solar-powered house in town. All sources of energy, including alternative energy sources, present problems such as unevenness of supply, and trade-offs such as less expense at the cost of convenience. Identify the greatest costs and benefits of the solar-powered house, and propose solutions to the problems or inconveniences you see.

Continued on next page →

Type of Knowledge	General Statement of Knowledge	Goal Statement	Sample Task
Declarative Knowledge (Information)	Generalizations proposed during the Constitutional Convention	Students will be able to propose a solution to a problem regarding political representation based on an understanding of issues raised during the Constitutional Convention and how they were resolved.	Poor nations may believe that they do not have strong enough voices at the U.N., but wealthy nations, who significantly impact trade and commerce in the world, likely believe that the strength of their influence should reflect this greater contribution. How might the structure of the U.N. be revised to accommodate both concerns? To solve this problem, use what you know of the ideas developed and agreements forged during the Constitutional Convention.
Procedural Knowledge (Mental and Psychomotor Skills, Strategies, and Processes)	The process of using a map and compass	Students will be able to navigate to a specified unfamiliar destination using a map and compass.	Each of your teams is going to a different spot in the field outside our classroom to find an object I have hidden. Use your school map and the compass to find your way there before class ends. Be prepared to explain how you overcame problems you encountered.
	The process of writing a story	Students will be able to create and resolve a conflict in an original story in a novel way.	Write a story that involves a conflict between good and evil in some way. Resolve the conflict in such a way that neither side has a decided victory.
	Correct pronunciation in a foreign language	Students will be able to solve a problem of pronunciation through making notes to self in an unfamiliar language about pronunciation.	You are to present a speech in the foreign language we have been studying, and you have had consistent problems pronouncing some of the words in the speech. How might you write out the speech for yourself to ensure that you say each word correctly?
	The process of portraying a character	Students will be able to solve acting challenges through an understanding of techniques used to project characters.	The character you've been selected to play is very old, something which you won't be for a very long time. Describe what physical techniques you'll use to make the audience believe that you are much older than you appear. What obstacles did this task present for you? How did you overcome them?

Verbs that teachers frequently use when designing problem-solving goals and tasks include the following:

- Solve
- How would you overcome
- Adapt

- Develop a strategy to
- Figure out a way to
- How will you reach your goal under these conditions

Assessment tasks for problem-solving goals typically require fairly extensive constructed-response formats.

Experimenting Goals and Tasks

Experimenting goals require students to generate and test hypotheses about a specific physical or psychological phenomenon. A critical feature of experimenting goals is that the data are newly collected by the student. That is, students must use data that they have generated. Table 3.16 depicts experimenting goals and tasks involving declarative and procedural knowledge.

Table 3.16 Experimenting Goals and Tasks

Type of Knowledge	General Statement of Knowledge	Goal Statement	Sample Task
Declarative Knowledge (Information)	Details about a specific current event	Students will be able to make and test predictions about how selected events might be viewed by members of the community.	We have been talking about the new plan for building an airport outside of town. How do you think different people in our community are reacting to this plan? Provide reasons for your prediction, and then see if you were right by reading the selection of editorials provided.
	Information about gender relations	Students will be able to test the idea that girls and boys tend to be friends with people of the same gender.	Write down observations about who girls and boys play with at recess. Look at your observations and those of your neighbor, and determine if it is true or false that girls and boys tend to be friends with people of the same gender.
	Details about a specific technological innovation	Students will be able to generate and test a hypothesis that demonstrates an understanding of the possible impact of a recent technology on society.	Select a development in technology that has occurred in the last twenty years. For example, you might select the iPod. Based on what we have discussed about how such changes impact society, develop a hypothesis about how that technology has had an impact on people's lives. Then gather information that will directly test your hypothesis.
	Principles of design in art	Students will be able to generate and test a hypothesis regarding design principles and their effects on the viewer.	Select three different visual structures that, according to the design principles we've been studying, can have effects on the viewer such as a sense of balance, anxiety, or rhythm. Create simple drawings that you believe exemplify each structure, and find out if you are successful in communicating what you intend. For example, survey your classmates to find out which drawing represents which effect. Decide, based on the results, if you can improve your design.

Continued on next page →

Type of Knowledge	General Statement of Knowledge	Goal Statement	Sample Task
Procedural Knowledge (Mental and Psychomotor Skills, Strategies, and Processes)	Skills and strategies for measuring time	Students will be able to make and test basic predictions about where the sun and earth will be in relation to one another when we enter the next season.	We have been studying the rotation of the earth around the sun and how that rotation affects the seasons. When we move into the next season, where will the earth be in its orbit? Explain your reasoning, and check your prediction using the class model of the solar system.
	The process of keyboarding	Students will be able to generate and test a hypothesis about the likely usefulness of a specific keyboarding invention in a specific situation.	The QWERTY keyboard was designed to slow down typists because early mechanical typewriters were not well designed and would jam easily. Computer keyboards don't jam, though, and August Dvorak designed a keyboard to make typing more comfortable and a little faster. Compare the two keyboard designs, and generate a hypothesis that tests the usefulness of his design.
	Personal exercise techniques	Students will be able to generate and test a hypothesis regarding the conditions that are optimal for personal exercise.	Keep a log of your exercise. Note the time of day, how long before and after a meal, the type of meal, how effective the exercise seemed to be, and whatever information you think might be helpful. At the end of a three-week period, review the data, and generate a hypothesis about the best conditions for exercise. Implement an exercise plan based on your hypothesis. After three weeks of your new plan, compare the two logs.
	Strategies for solving a specific type of mathematics problem	Students will be able to generate a hypothesis regarding the best math strategies to use in solving a specific estimation problem and test their relative effectiveness.	Imagine a scenario in which you have a limited amount of money and are in the grocery store adding items to a shopping cart. You don't have a calculator, so you've got to keep a running total in your head of the cost of the items as you add them. Develop two or more techniques for mentally estimating or calculating the totals as you go. You can even develop techniques that use items in your cart to help keep track of the running total. How would you go about testing the effectiveness of your approach?

Verbs that teachers frequently use when designing experimenting goals and tasks include the following:

- Experiment

- Generate and test

- Test the idea that

- What would happen if

- How would you test that

- How would you determine if

- How can this be explained

- Based on the experiment, what can be predicted

Assessment tasks for experimenting goals typically require fairly extensive constructed-response formats.

Investigating Goals and Tasks

Investigating goals require students to examine a past, present, or future situation. Investigating goals are similar to experimenting goals in that they involve the gathering and testing of data. However, the data used in investigating goals are not gathered by direct observation on the part of the student as they are in experimenting goals. Instead, the data used in investigating goals are assertions and opinions that have been made by others. Investigating may be likened more to investigative reporting, whereas experimenting may be likened more to pure scientific inquiry. Table 3.17 depicts investigating goals and tasks for declarative and procedural knowledge.

Table 3.17 Investigating Goals and Tasks

Type of Knowledge	General Statement of Knowledge	Goal Statement	Sample Task
Declarative Knowledge (Information)	Information about nutrition	Students will be able to investigate the relationship between diet and health in humans.	Research two popular diets (The Atkins diet and the Zone diet) and their effects on overall health.
	Information about gravity	Students will describe what would happen if there was no gravity on earth.	Research the effects of gravity on the human body and what happens to the human body in space. What do you think would happen if there was no gravity on earth?
	Information about the Roman Empire	Students will be able to provide a cause and effect analysis of the rise and fall of the Roman Empire.	When researching the Roman Empire, pay special attention to the events that allowed its rise and the major factors that led to its demise.
	Information about calculus	Students will be able to investigate the origins of calculus.	Who created calculus? What need did it originally fill, and what kinds of math were used to create it? Research and compare different theories.
Procedural Knowledge (Mental and Psychomotor Skills, Strategies, and Processes)	The process and rules regarding a specific sport	Students will be able to investigate how changes in a sport's rules can have impact on play.	Identify a rule change in the past decade of professional basketball that has had an impact on play call and/or play execution. What was the intention of the rule change, and has it been effective?

Continued on next page →

Type of Knowledge	General Statement of Knowledge	Goal Statement	Sample Task
Procedural Knowledge (Mental and Psychomotor Skills, Strategies, and Processes)	The process of creating a contour map	Students will be able to investigate who created contour maps and what needs they fulfill.	Who created the first contour map, and what need did it fill? Are there more sophisticated maps that have been created since?
	The use of internet databases	Students will be able to investigate the early origins of internet databases.	We have been using a variety of types of internet databases. In fact, the internet has not been around that long. What were some of the earlier versions of internet databases? How have they changed?
	The process of modeling and solving real-world problems using recurrent relations	Students will be able to investigate the origins of the concept of recurrent relations.	We have been studying various uses of recurrent relationships to model real-world problems. Using the internet and other sources, identify the origins of this idea. Who first started using the term *recurrent relationships*? What types of real-world problems were they dealing with?

Verbs that teachers frequently use when designing investigating goals and tasks include the following:

- Investigate

- Research

- Find out about

- Take a position on

- What are the differing features of

- How did this happen

- Why did this happen

- What would have happened if

Assessment tasks for investigating goals typically require fairly extensive constructed-response formats.

In summary, there are four types of knowledge utilization goals: decision-making goals, problem-solving goals, experimenting goals, and investigating goals. Exercise 3.4 provides practice in identifying various types of knowledge utilization goals. (See page 61 for a reproducible of this exercise and page 112 for a reproducible answer sheet. Visit **marzanoresearch.com/classroomstrategies** to download all the exercises and answers in this book.)

Exercise 3.4
Identifying Different Types of Knowledge Utilization Goals

Following are some examples of goal statements at the knowledge utilization level. For each, identify whether it is more closely a decision-making, problem-solving, experimenting, or investigating goal statement. Keep in mind that there is some fluidity and overlap between and among the types of knowledge utilization goals.

1. Students will be able to select the best brushstroke for creating a composition that focuses on texture.

   Decision Making   Problem Solving   Experimenting   Investigating

2. Students will be able to design an alternative mode of transportation with attention to energy efficiency.

   Decision Making   Problem Solving   Experimenting   Investigating

3. Students will be able to discuss hypothetical conclusions to the Vietnam War if President Kennedy had not been assassinated.

   Decision Making   Problem Solving   Experimenting   Investigating

4. Students will be able to generate and test ideas about how to win a tennis game.

   Decision Making   Problem Solving   Experimenting   Investigating

5. Students will be able to test what will happen to water if the surrounding temperature changes.

   Decision Making   Problem Solving   Experimenting   Investigating

6. Students will be able to select the most suitable format for a persuasive essay based on specific criteria.

   Decision Making   Problem Solving   Experimenting   Investigating

7. Students will be able to research and take a position on a current political issue.

   Decision Making   Problem Solving   Experimenting   Investigating

8. Students will be able to determine the probability of a specific outcome given a set of conditions.

   Decision Making   Problem Solving   Experimenting   Investigating

9. Students will be able to develop a strategy for collecting data schoolwide given a limited period of time.

   Decision Making   Problem Solving   Experimenting   Investigating

10. Students will be able to research and make a presentation on the life of an influential American leader.

    Decision Making   Problem Solving   Experimenting   Investigating

Summary

One of the key considerations in designing learning goals is level of difficulty. By designing goals at different difficulty levels, the teacher can ensure that each student is challenged without being overwhelmed. This is the core of effective differentiation. The four levels of cognition outlined in the New Taxonomy (retrieval, comprehension, analysis, and knowledge utilization) allow teachers to easily construct appropriate goals for every student as well as corresponding assessment items and tasks. Appendix C (page 123) provides a listing of the terms and phrases commonly used when designing assessment tasks for learning goals at the various levels of the New Taxonomy.

Exercise 3.1

Identifying Different Types of Retrieval Goals

Following are some examples of goal statements at the retrieval level. For each, identify whether it is more closely a recognizing, recalling, or executing goal statement. Keep in mind that there is some fluidity and overlap between and among the types of retrieval goals.

1. Students will be able to identify from a list the steps involved in photosynthesis.
   Recognizing   Recalling   Executing

2. Students will be able to play a piece of music.
   Recognizing   Recalling   Executing

3. Students will be able to name six prominent world political leaders.
   Recognizing   Recalling   Executing

4. Students will be able to list the continents.
   Recognizing   Recalling   Executing

5. Students will be able to identify accurate vs. inaccurate information about presidential candidates.
   Recognizing   Recalling   Executing

6. Students will be able to list the major combatant nations of World War II.
   Recognizing   Recalling   Executing

7. Students will be able to select mammals from a list of animals.
   Recognizing   Recalling   Executing

8. Students will be able to identify examples of complete sentences.
   Recognizing   Recalling   Executing

9. Students will be able to list examples of proper nouns.
   Recognizing   Recalling   Executing

10. Students will be able to perform addition using two-digit numbers.
    Recognizing   Recalling   Executing

Exercise 3.2

Identifying Different Types of Comprehension Goals

Following are some examples of goal statements at the comprehension level. For each, identify whether it is more closely an integrating or symbolizing goal statement. Keep in mind that there is some fluidity and overlap between and among the comprehension goals.

1. Students will be able to describe the major components of an organism's behavior cycle.

   Integrating   Symbolizing

2. Students will be able to create a flowchart that shows the steps involved in tying a shoe.

   Integrating   Symbolizing

3. Students will be able to describe the key reasons eating healthy food provides the body with more energy.

   Integrating   Symbolizing

4. Students will be able to describe the major contributions to society made by Dr. Martin Luther King, Jr.

   Integrating   Symbolizing

5. Students will be able to summarize the results of a scientific experiment.

   Integrating   Symbolizing

6. Students will be able to diagram the transitions between key ideas in an expository text.

   Integrating   Symbolizing

7. Students will be able to create pictorial representations of the cause and effect sequence of an event in history.

   Integrating   Symbolizing

8. Students will be able to paraphrase the important points made by a speaker.

   Integrating   Symbolizing

9. Students will be able to use manipulatives to demonstrate the process of multiplication.

   Integrating   Symbolizing

10. Students will be able to describe the defining aspects of a musical genre.

    Integrating   Symbolizing

Exercise 3.3

Identifying Different Types of Analysis Goals

Following are some examples of goal statements at the analysis level. For each, identify whether it is more closely a matching, classifying, analyzing errors, generalizing, or specifying goal statement. Keep in mind that there is some fluidity and overlap between and among the types of analysis goals.

1. Students will be able to organize a group of sentences into the following categories: simple, compound, complex.
   Matching   Classifying   Analyzing Errors   Generalizing   Specifying

2. Given a group of statements, students will be able to generate conclusions that flow from them.
   Matching   Classifying   Analyzing Errors   Generalizing   Specifying

3. Students will be able to compare and contrast classical, romantic, and modern styles of music.
   Matching   Classifying   Analyzing Errors   Generalizing   Specifying

4. Students will be able to develop an office floor plan based on specific principles of communication and justify its layout.
   Matching   Classifying   Analyzing Errors   Generalizing   Specifying

5. Students will describe how their observations are similar or dissimilar to others' observations.
   Matching   Classifying   Analyzing Errors   Generalizing   Specifying

6. Students will be able to categorize types of statistical calculations according to their use.
   Matching   Classifying   Analyzing Errors   Generalizing   Specifying

7. Students will be able to identify and correct logical errors in a written argument.
   Matching   Classifying   Analyzing Errors   Generalizing   Specifying

8. Students will be able to infer the global implications of a proposed energy technology.
   Matching   Classifying   Analyzing Errors   Generalizing   Specifying

9. Students will be able to judge what colors would best enhance a workspace.
   Matching   Classifying   Analyzing Errors   Generalizing   Specifying

10. Students will be able to identify problems in the flow of their writing and correct them.
    Matching   Classifying   Analyzing Errors   Generalizing   Specifying

Exercise 3.4

Identifying Different Types of Knowledge Utilization Goals

Following are some examples of goal statements at the knowledge utilization level. For each, identify whether it is more closely a decision-making, problem-solving, experimenting, or investigating goal statement. Keep in mind that there is some fluidity and overlap between and among the types of knowledge utilization goals.

1. Students will be able to select the best brushstroke for creating a composition that focuses on texture.
   Decision Making   Problem Solving   Experimenting   Investigating

2. Students will be able to design an alternative mode of transportation with attention to energy efficiency.
   Decision Making   Problem Solving   Experimenting   Investigating

3. Students will be able to discuss hypothetical conclusions to the Vietnam War if President Kennedy had not been assassinated.
   Decision Making   Problem Solving   Experimenting   Investigating

4. Students will be able to generate and test ideas about how to win a tennis game.
   Decision Making   Problem Solving   Experimenting   Investigating

5. Students will be able to test what will happen to water if the surrounding temperature changes.
   Decision Making   Problem Solving   Experimenting   Investigating

6. Students will be able to select the most suitable format for a persuasive essay based on specific criteria.
   Decision Making   Problem Solving   Experimenting   Investigating

7. Students will be able to research and take a position on a current political issue.
   Decision Making   Problem Solving   Experimenting   Investigating

8. Students will be able to determine the probability of a specific outcome given a set of conditions.
   Decision Making   Problem Solving   Experimenting   Investigating

9. Students will be able to develop a strategy for collecting data schoolwide given a limited period of time.
   Decision Making   Problem Solving   Experimenting   Investigating

10. Students will be able to research and make a presentation on the life of an influential American leader.
    Decision Making   Problem Solving   Experimenting   Investigating

Chapter 4

ORGANIZING LEARNING GOALS INTO A SCALE

In chapter 3, we presented a framework that allows teachers to design learning goals at four levels of difficulty: retrieval, comprehension, analysis, and knowledge utilization. Recall from the discussion at the beginning of that chapter that the reasons a teacher would want to design goals at different levels of complexity are twofold: (1) for goals to be effective instructional tools, they must be challenging but attainable by students; and (2) given that students in any classroom will have differing levels of understanding regarding a topic in a unit of instruction, the teacher must design multiple goals at different levels of complexity to meet the "challenging but attainable" criterion. We also briefly introduced the notion of organizing goals into a scale (see table 3.2, page 27). This chapter describes how to organize learning goals into a rubric or scale using the framework provided in chapter 3.

Identify a Target Goal for the Class

The process of creating multiple goals organized in a scale begins by identifying a target goal for a unit of instruction. As we saw in chapter 2, these goals must usually be gleaned from state standards documents, district standards documents, or district lists of essential learner outcomes. Again, as we saw in chapter 2, a teacher must keep in mind whether the goal involves declarative knowledge or procedural knowledge and then write the goal in an appropriate format. To illustrate, a high school social studies teacher might identify the following learning goal:

> Students will be able to create a flowchart depicting the rise and fall of Napoleon.

This represents the target for all students in the class. In effect, the teacher is establishing this as the criterion for success in her unit—all students will be able to create a flowchart depicting the rise and fall of Napoleon.

The next step is to determine the level of complexity of the target learning goal using the New Taxonomy framework described in chapter 3. That taxonomy is again depicted in table 4.1 (page 64).

It is important to keep in mind that level 1 through level 4 represent a hierarchy. However, *within* levels of the New Taxonomy, the types of goals do not represent a hierarchy (with one notable exception). For example, consider the level 4 knowledge utilization goals. Decision making is not more complex than problem solving, problem solving is not more complex than experimenting, and so on. All four of

Table 4.1 Four Levels of the New Taxonomy

Level of Difficulty	Mental Process
Level 4: Knowledge Utilization	Decision Making
	Problem Solving
	Experimenting
	Investigating
Level 3: Analysis	Matching
	Classifying
	Analyzing Errors
	Generalizing
	Specifying
Level 2: Comprehension	Integrating
	Symbolizing
Level 1: Retrieval	Recognizing
	Recalling
	Executing

the cognitive processes simply represent different ways students might use knowledge. This nonhierarchical structure within levels of the New Taxonomy applies to all levels *except* level 1, retrieval. Within retrieval, executing is more complex than recalling, and recalling is more complex than recognizing.

Armed with an understanding of the New Taxonomy, teachers can identify the level of complexity of the target goal. In the preceding case, the target goal involves symbolizing, which is an aspect of comprehension—level 2 in the New Taxonomy. The teacher would next construct a goal at a lower level. It is important to note that there are no hard and fast rules for designing goals at a lower level. The lower-level goals should be selected on the basis of what makes the most sense instructionally. In this case, the teacher might identify the following recognizing goal:

> Students will be able to identify accurate statements about the rise and fall of Napoleon.

At this level, the teacher does not expect students to describe the most important aspects of Napoleon's rise and fall or put that information into an abstract form; however, the teacher does expect students to recognize accurate statements about Napoleon's life. This involves the retrieval process of *recognizing*. The teacher could have selected a *recalling* goal like the following:

> Students will be able to describe some important events in Napoleon's life.

Here they are expected to describe some of the important events in Napoleon's life. This, of course, is more complex than simply recognizing accurate statements about Napoleon's life.

With a lower-level goal identified, the teacher would next design a higher-level goal such as the following:

> Students will be able to compare and contrast Napoleon and other military and political leaders.

At this level, students are expected to distinguish between important and unimportant information about Napoleon, as well as apply that information to make connections between Napoleon and other military and political leaders. This learning goal involves the level 3 (analysis) process of matching.

Again, the decision as to the level of the New Taxonomy that will be used should be instructionally based—which learning goals will best serve the students' needs? The teacher could have decided to focus on a knowledge utilization goal such as the following:

Students will be able to determine the possible alternatives Napoleon was considering when he decided to invade Russia.

This is a decision-making goal from level 4 in the New Taxonomy. It requires a deeper level of understanding than the previous analysis goal.

The preceding examples involve goals that belong to different levels of the New Taxonomy: retrieval, comprehension, analysis, and knowledge utilization. Keep in mind that this is not always the case, especially when procedural knowledge is the focus of instruction. To illustrate, consider the following set of procedural goals:

Target learning goal: Students will be able to write a persuasive essay using appropriate sources within a format provided by the teacher.

Simpler goal: Students will be able to use elements of persuasive writing in highly structured assignments.

More complex goal: Students will be able to select and use the most appropriate format for a persuasive essay on a chosen topic and use multiple sources to address an argument and any possible counterarguments.

The target learning goal involves executing the procedure of writing a persuasive essay using appropriate resources and a format identified by the teacher. This is an executing goal. The simpler goal also involves executing a procedure, but the procedure is much less complex. Here students are not expected to execute the entire procedure for writing a persuasive essay, but they are expected to execute parts of the procedure within the context of assignments that are highly structured. The more complex goal also involves executing the procedure of writing a persuasive essay; however, this procedure has added components to the initial target procedure (the initial learning goal). Now the students must demonstrate competence that exceeds the target goal by selecting the most appropriate format for a persuasive essay, using multiple sources and addressing any possible counterarguments.

With procedural knowledge, then, the expectation for students is that they can perform more complex versions of the procedure as opposed to using more complex aspects of the New Taxonomy. To illustrate again, consider the following learning goal involving procedural knowledge:

Students will be able to multiply a two-digit number by another two-digit number.

A simpler goal would be as follows:

Students will be able to multiply a two-digit number by a one-digit number.

A more complex goal would be as follows:

Students will be able to multiply a number with three or more digits by a two-digit number.

In this set of goals, the underlying procedure is multiplying multiple-digit numbers. However, from level to level, the number of digits changes in the multiplier and the multiplicand.

Exercise 4.1 provides some practice in ordering goals by level of difficulty. (See page 75 for a reproducible of this exercise and page 114 for a reproducible answer sheet. Visit **marzanoresearch.com/ classroomstrategies** to download all the exercises and answers in this book.)

Exercise 4.1
Ordering Goals by Level of Difficulty

In each of the following sets of learning goals, there is a target goal and goals that are above (or more difficult) and below (or simpler) in difficulty or complexity. Order each set by numbering them 1, 2, or 3, where 1 represents the simplest (or least difficult) goal.

A.   Students will be able to discuss the body's most important dietary needs.

Students will be able to recognize healthy versus unhealthy foods given a list.

Students will be able to discuss what would happen to the body if one of its needs was not met. (For example, what would happen if the body received no calcium for an extended period of time?)

B.   Students will be able to design complex word problems based on given mathematical equations.

Students will be able to translate between simple word problems and mathematical equations.

Students will be able to recognize accurate statements about the mathematical processes embedded in word problems.

C.   Students will be able to combine simple, compound, and compound-complex sentences fluently.

Students will be able to write a simple sentence with a subject and a predicate.

Students will be able to write compound-complex sentences in isolation.

D.   Students will be able to make simple measurements in standard units.

Students will be able to convert between standard and nonstandard unit measurements.

Students will be able to make simple conversions within standard or nonstandard unit measurements.

E.   Students will be able to discuss the key aspects of Roosevelt's foreign policy during World War II.

Students will be able to recognize accurate statements about Roosevelt's foreign policy during World War II.

Students will be able to compare the successes and failures of different presidents' foreign policies during times of conflict.

Organize Learning Goals Into a Scale

A clear learning goal that is the target of instruction, along with a goal that is more complex and a goal that is simpler, can be organized into a rubric or scale. Here we use the scale described in the books *Classroom Assessment and Grading That Work* (Marzano, 2006) and *Making Standards Useful in the Classroom* (Marzano & Haystead, 2008). A simpler version of the scale was presented in chapter 3 (see table 3.2, page 27). The complete scale is depicted in table 4.2.

To understand the scale in table 4.2, we start with the whole-point scores. It's easiest to understand the scale by starting with the score 3.0 content. It is the target learning goal. That is, when using the scale, a teacher would insert the target goal for the class in score 3.0. The next whole-point score down is 2.0. The simpler learning goal would go here. The next whole-point score up from the target learning goal (3.0) is 4.0. The more complex learning goal goes there.

The three learning goals, then, designed by a teacher, occupy score values 2.0, 3.0, and 4.0, respectively. But there are two other whole-point score values: 1.0 and 0.0. These values do not represent new content, but they do represent different levels of competence. Score 1.0 indicates

Table 4.2 Complete Scale for Learning Goals

Score 4.0	More complex learning goal
Score 3.5	In addition to score 3.0 performance, partial success at score 4.0 content
Score 3.0	Target learning goal
Score 2.5	No major errors or omissions regarding score 2.0 content, and partial success at score 3.0 content
Score 2.0	Simpler learning goal
Score 1.5	Partial success at score 2.0 content, and major errors or omissions regarding score 3.0 content
Score 1.0	With help, partial success at score 2.0 content and score 3.0 content
Score 0.5	With help, partial success at score 2.0 content but not at score 3.0 content
Score 0.0	Even with help, no success

that the student does not demonstrate competence in any of the learning goals when working independently. However, with help, the student has partial success at the score 2.0 and score 3.0 content (the target learning goal and the simpler goal). Score 0.0 indicates that even with help, the student has no success at the 3.0 or 2.0 content. Thus, the target goal, a related simpler goal, and a related, more complex goal can be organized into a scale with five whole-point scores (0.0, 1.0, 2.0, 3.0, and 4.0).

Next, we examine the half-point scores (.05, 1.5, 2.5, and 3.5). Again, it is useful to begin with the target goal—score 3.0 content. A score of 2.5 means that the student has success at the score 2.0 (the simpler learning goal) content and has partial success at the score 3.0 content (the target learning goal). A score of 3.5 indicates that a student has success at the 3.0 content (the target learning goal) and partial success at the 4.0 content (the more complex learning goal). A score of 1.5 indicates that a student has partial success at the score 2.0 content (the simpler learning goal). Finally, a score of 0.5 indicates that *with help*, a student has partial success at the score 2.0 content.

The generic scale in table 4.2 can be used to translate any hierarchal set of three goals into a scale that can be used to measure student progress. To illustrate, reconsider the following three learning goals regarding Napoleon:

> More complex goal: Students will be able to compare and contrast Napoleon and other military and political leaders.

> Target goal: Students will be able to create a flowchart depicting the rise and fall of Napoleon.

> Simpler goal: Students will be able to identify accurate statements about the rise and fall of Napoleon.

Again, it is useful to point out a format change. You will note that the goal statements in table 4.3 (page 68) do not all include the generic stem, "Students will be able to." This is common when organizing goal statements into scale format. Although you could use the generic stem, you should feel free to find a format that best conveys student expectations. Whatever format you choose, however, should make clear the distinction between declarative and procedural knowledge.

Table 4.3 The Full Scale for These Three Learning Goals

Scale for Napoleon, Grade 8	
Score 4.0	**The student:** • Compares and contrasts Napoleon and other military and political leaders. **No major errors or omissions regarding the score 4.0 content**
Score 3.5	In addition to score 3.0 performance, partial success at score 4.0 content
Score 3.0	**The student:** • Makes a flowchart depicting the rise and fall of Napoleon (for example, creates an illustrated flowchart that includes Napoleon's 1799 coup d'etat, his major military achievements, and his final invasion of Russia). **No major errors or omissions regarding the score 3.0 content**
Score 2.5	No major errors or omissions regarding score 2.0 content and partial success at score 3.0 content

Score 2.0	**The student:**
	
	• Recalls accurate information about the rise and fall of Napoleon, such as:
	  • He was not French by birth and never mastered the language.
	  • His first position of significant military command was with France's Army of Italy.
	  • He was imprisoned and then exiled to the island of St. Helena in 1815.
	
	No major errors or omissions regarding the score 2.0 content

Score 1.5	Partial success at score 2.0 content, and major errors or omissions regarding score 3.0 content
Score 1.0	**With help, partial success at score 2.0 content and score 3.0 content**
Score 0.5	With help, partial success at score 2.0 content, but not at score 3.0 content
Score 0.0	**Even with help, no success**

Table 4.4 depicts a scale that a second grade science teacher planning a unit on plants and animals might construct. Her target goal is for students to understand how plants and animals survive.

Table 4.4 Scale for a Second Grade Science Teacher

Score 4.0	**The student:** • Compares the different ways in which plants and animals breathe and find nourishment (for example, knows that plants use their roots and leaves to take in air and food while animals use their lungs to breathe and their digestive systems to obtain nourishment). **No major errors or omissions regarding the score 4.0 content**
Score 3.5	In addition to score 3.0 performance, partial success at score 4.0 content
Score 3.0	**The student:** • Discusses what plants and animals need to survive (for example, knows that no living thing can live without air, food, and water). **No major errors or omissions regarding the score 3.0 content**
Score 2.5	No major errors or omissions regarding score 2.0 content and partial success at score 3.0 content

Score 2.0	**The student:**
	• Recognizes and recalls specific terminology, such as:
	   • Plant
	   • Animal
	   • Survival
	• Recalls accurate information about the survival needs of animals and plants such as:
	   • Both animals and plants need food, water, and air to survive.
	   • Plants absorb nutrients and air through their roots and leaves.
	   • Animals use respiration (lungs) to breathe and digestion to process nutrients.
	No major errors or omissions regarding the score 2.0 content

Score 1.5	Partial success at score 2.0 content, and major errors or omissions regarding score 3.0 content
Score 1.0	**With help, partial success at score 2.0 content and score 3.0 content**
Score 0.5	With help, partial success at score 2.0 content, but not at score 3.0 content
Score 0.0	**Even with help, no success**

Table 4.5 depicts a scale that a high school mathematics teacher might design.

Table 4.5 Scale for High School Mathematics

Score 4.0	**The student:** • Analyzes a solution to a system of linear equations for errors. **No major errors or omissions regarding the score 4.0 content**
Score 3.5	In addition to score 3.0 performance, partial success at score 4.0 content
Score 3.0	**The student:** • Solves a system of linear equations algebraically or by using matrices. **No major errors or omissions regarding the score 3.0 content**
Score 2.5	No major errors or omissions regarding score 2.0 content and partial success at score 3.0 content

Score 2.0	**The student:**
	• Recognizes and recalls specific terminology, such as:
	   • Linear equation
	   • Matrix
	• Recalls information about linear equations and how they are solved such as:
	   • A system of linear equations can be solved algebraically.
	   • A system of linear equations can be solved using matrices.
	   • A system of linear equations is a collection of linear equations with the same variables.
	No major errors or omissions regarding the score 2.0 content

Score 1.5	Partial success at score 2.0 content, and major errors or omissions regarding score 3.0 content
Score 1.0	**With help, partial success at score 2.0 content and score 3.0 content**
Score 0.5	With help, partial success at score 2.0 content, but not at score 3.0 content
Score 0.0	**Even with help, no success**

Exercise 4.2 provides some practice in designing scales around learning goals. (See page 76 for a reproducible of this exercise and page 116 for a reproducible answer sheet. Visit **marzanoresearch** **.com/classroomstrategies** to download all the exercises and answers in this book.)

Exercise 4.2
Designing a Scale

	Using the following form, design a scale for a recent goal you have addressed in class by filling in the score 4.0, 3.0, and 2.0 content.	
Score 4.0	The student: • No major errors or omissions regarding the score 4.0 content	
Score 3.5	In addition to score 3.0 performance, partial success at score 4.0 content	
Score 3.0	The student: • No major errors or omissions regarding the score 3.0 content	
Score 2.5	No major errors or omissions regarding score 2.0 content, and partial success at score 3.0 content	
Score 2.0	The student: • No major errors or omissions regarding the score 2.0 content	
Score 1.5	Partial success at score 2.0 content, but major errors or omissions regarding score 3.0 content	
Score 1.0	With help, partial success at score 2.0 content and score 3.0 content	
Score 0.5	With help, partial success at score 2.0 content, but not at score 3.0 content	
Score 0.0	Even with help, no success	

Consider Noncognitive Goals

The learning goals traditionally defined by teachers and administrators in K–12 education are cognitive in nature in that they focus on academic content. However, as indicated in the research and theory chapter, there is growing interest in supplementing these learning goals with goals that are noncognitive in nature. Noncognitive goals often refer to behaviors and/or attitudes that are not explicitly tied to content. For example, social skills and self-awareness goals are important parts of learning, yet they do not clearly incorporate any specific content. They are noncognitive in the sense that they do not involve levels of processing (cognition) in the same way that content-related material does, but instead involve skills that are exercised in the social and interpersonal world. Common areas for which teachers write noncognitive goals include the following:

- Self-awareness/self-control
- Academic self-concept
- Empathy/respect
- Social awareness and response
- Goal setting
- Emotional awareness

- Study skills

- Team building

- Problem solving

- Adaptability

Learning goals and scales for noncognitive goals can be written just as they can be written for cognitive goals. Table 4.6 depicts a scale for the skill of goal setting, which is a commonly identified noncognitive goal.

The target goal in table 4.6—score 3.0 content—involves articulating a personal goal and mapping out steps to complete it. This requires execution of the procedure of goal setting. The more complex goal (score 4.0 content) requires students to execute a more complex version of the procedure. The students must examine progress toward the goal and make necessary changes. The simpler goal (score 2.0 content) requires students to execute a simpler version of the procedure. In this case, to obtain a score of 2.0, they must set a specific goal in a specific situation. The goal would be short term in nature and not require extensive planning. Score 2.0 also requires students to recognize or recall some basic terminology.

Table 4.6 Goal-Setting Scale

Score 4.0	The student: • Maps progress toward a goal and makes any necessary changes (for example, knows that his or her progression toward a personal goal has been lagging because of lack of effort). **No major errors or omissions regarding the score 4.0 content**
Score 3.5	In addition to score 3.0 performance, partial success at score 4.0 content
Score 3.0	The student: • Sets a goal and maps out a plan to achieve that goal (for example, the student picks out an area of personal weakness in writing, sets a goal to master a skill [such as active voice] by the end of the unit or term, and discusses how he or she thinks that goal can be accomplished). **No major errors or omissions regarding the score 3.0 content**
Score 2.5	No major errors or omissions regarding score 2.0 content, and partial success at score 3.0 content

Score 2.0	The student:
	
	• Recognizes and recalls specific terminology, such as:
	  • Goal
	  • Progression
	• Performs basic processes, such as:
	  • Setting a (short-term) goal for a given lesson or a given situation (for example, given the topic of writing a persuasive essay, the student sets the goal of writing an introductory and concluding paragraph).
	
	No major errors or omissions regarding the score 2.0 content

Score 1.5	Partial success at score 2.0 content, and major errors or omissions regarding score 3.0 content
Score 1.0	**With help, partial success at score 2.0 content and score 3.0 content**
Score 0.5	With help, partial success at score 2.0 content, but not score 3.0 content
Score 0.0	**Even with help, no success**

Table 4.7 depicts a scale for a noncognitive goal regarding emotional awareness. The target goal in table 4.7—score 3.0 content—requires students to describe their physical reactions to various emotions. This might be considered an integration goal (a form of comprehension) because students must discern the major characteristics of their physical reactions to various emotions. The more complex goal (score 4.0 content) requires students to group their physical reactions into designated categories. This is a matching goal (a form of analysis). The simpler goal (score 2.0 content) requires students to recall statements about general reactions to emotions and to recognize or recall some basic terminology (forms of retrieval).

As shown in table 4.6 and table 4.7, teachers can design scales for noncognitive goals in the same way as for cognitive goals. However, there are some important differences between cognitive goals and noncognitive goals. As we have seen, assessment tasks can be designed fairly easily for cognitive goals at each level of the New Taxonomy. In some situations, the types of assessments that are used for cognitive goals can be used for noncognitive goals. Consider the scale for emotional awareness (table 4.7). For score 2.0 content, a teacher might ask students to respond to a series of multiple-choice

Table 4.7 Emotional Awareness

Score 4.0	The student: <ul><li>Categorizes emotions as either frequent or infrequent and discusses why (for example, describes how he or she gets mad often for no reason and acknowledges that this is not a reaction his or her friends have).</li></ul> **No major errors or omissions regarding the score 4.0 content**
Score 3.5	In addition to score 3.0 performance, partial success at score 4.0 content
Score 3.0	The student: <ul><li>Describes his or her physical reactions to various emotions (for example, describes that when he or she gets angry, his or her hands physically shake).</li></ul> **No major errors or omissions regarding the score 3.0 content**
Score 2.5	No major errors or omissions regarding score 2.0 content, and partial success at score 3.0 content
Score 2.0	The student: <ul><li>Recognizes and recalls specific terminology, such as:<ul><li>Emotion</li><li>Reaction</li></ul></li><li>Recalls general information about emotions such as:<ul><li>People react to their emotions in physically apparent ways.</li><li>Emotions are usually caused by a triggering event (for example, says, "I was sad because my best friend moved away").</li><li>We usually have consistent physical reactions to our emotions, and those reactions can tell us how we are feeling.</li></ul></li></ul> **No major errors or omissions regarding the score 2.0 content**
Score 1.5	Partial knowledge of score 2.0 content, and major errors or omissions regarding score 3.0 content
Score 1.0	**With help, partial success at score 2.0 content and score 3.0 content**
Score 0.5	With help, partial success at score 2.0 content, but not at score 3.0 content
Score 0.0	**Even with help, no success**

or true/false items. For the score 3.0 content, the teacher might ask students to respond to an essay question like the following:

> Explain your physical reactions to each of the following emotions: happiness, sadness, fear, anger.

Similarly, for the score 4.0 content, the teacher might ask students to respond to an essay question like the following:

> Categorize each of the following emotions as either frequent or infrequent in your life, and explain your evidence for this: happiness, sadness, fear, anger.

Because emotional awareness involves information, it follows the same pattern as information in academic areas. Thus, it can be assessed in the same way as academic information. This is not the case, however, with the skill of goal setting, as depicted in table 4.6 (page 71). This noncognitive goal is procedural in nature. Additionally, it is difficult to design a task that would directly assess it at any one point in time. To assess this goal, the teacher would have to ask students to design a goal for a quarter or a semester and then observe their progress over time. Stated differently, the teacher must provide opportunities for students to demonstrate their ability to execute goal setting and then observe their doing so. This is the case with many noncognitive procedural goals—to assess students, the teacher must provide opportunities for students to reach the noncognitive procedural goal. Exercise 4.3 provides some practice at designing scales for noncognitive goals. (See page 77 for a reproducible of this exercise and page 117 for a reproducible answer sheet. Visit **marzanoresearch.com/ classroomstrategies** to download all the exercises and answers in this book.)

Exercise 4.3
Designing Noncognitive Scales

For each of the following scales, a noncognitive learning goal appears at the 3.0 score. Fill in the score 4.0 and 2.0 content.

1.

Score 4.0	The student: • No major errors or omissions regarding the score 4.0 content
Score 3.5	In addition to score 3.0 performance, partial success at score 4.0 content
Score 3.0	The student: • Discusses the consequences for breaking home and classroom rules. No major errors or omissions regarding the score 3.0 content
Score 2.5	No major errors or omissions regarding score 2.0 content, and partial success at score 3.0 content
Score 2.0	The student: • No major errors or omissions regarding the score 2.0 content
Score 1.5	Partial success at score 2.0 content, but major errors or omissions regarding score 3.0 content
Score 1.0	With help, partial success at score 2.0 content and score 3.0 content
Score 0.5	With help, partial success at score 2.0 content, but not at score 3.0 content
Score 0.0	Even with help, no success

Continued on next page →

2.

Score 4.0	The student: • No major errors or omissions regarding the score 4.0 content
Score 3.5	In addition to score 3.0 performance, partial success at score 4.0 content
Score 3.0	The student: • Picks up on and utilizes appropriate nonverbal language. No major errors or omissions regarding the score 3.0 content
Score 2.5	No major errors or omissions regarding score 2.0 content, and partial success at score 3.0 content
Score 2.0	The student: • No major errors or omissions regarding the score 2.0 content
Score 1.5	Partial success at score 2.0 content, but major errors or omissions regarding score 3.0 content
Score 1.0	With help, partial success at score 2.0 content and score 3.0 content
Score 0.5	With help, partial success at score 2.0 content, but not at score 3.0 content
Score 0.0	Even with help, no success

3.

Score 4.0	The student: • No major errors or omissions regarding the score 4.0 content
Score 3.5	In addition to score 3.0 performance, partial success at score 4.0 content
Score 3.0	The student: • Includes others in class assignments or games. No major errors or omissions regarding the score 3.0 content
Score 2.5	No major errors or omissions regarding score 2.0 content, and partial success at score 3.0 content
Score 2.0	The student: • No major errors or omissions regarding the score 2.0 content
Score 1.5	Partial success at score 2.0 content, but major errors or omissions regarding score 3.0 content
Score 1.0	With help, partial success at score 2.0 content and score 3.0 content
Score 0.5	With help, partial success at score 2.0 content, but not at score 3.0 content
Score 0.0	Even with help, no success

Summary

This chapter began with a discussion of the need for learning goals to be challenging to students but attainable by them. This poses a problem because students in a classroom will typically be at different levels of understanding or skill regarding any learning goal. The solution is to design multiple learning goals that address varying levels of difficulty. Once a teacher has identified a target learning goal for students as well as a goal that is simpler and a goal that is more complex, creating a rubric or scale is possible. The 0–4 scale presented in this chapter enables teachers to closely estimate a student's level of knowledge or skill by assigning the target goal to score 3.0, the simpler goal to score 2.0, and the more complex goal to score 4.0. In addition to academic goals, teachers can use this scale with noncognitive goals. By setting and assessing both cognitive and noncognitive goals designed to appropriately challenge every student in the class, teachers can obtain a comprehensive view of students' progress in multiple areas.

Exercise 4.1

Ordering Goals by Level of Difficulty

In each of the following sets of learning goals, there is a target goal and goals that are above (or more difficult) and below (or simpler) in difficulty or complexity. Order each set by numbering them 1, 2, or 3, where 1 represents the simplest (or least difficult) goal.

A. Students will be able to discuss the body's most important dietary needs.

Students will be able to recognize healthy versus unhealthy foods given a list.

Students will be able to discuss what would happen to the body if one of its needs was not met. (For example, what would happen if the body received no calcium for an extended period of time?)

B. Students will be able to design complex word problems based on given mathematical equations.

Students will be able to translate between simple word problems and mathematical equations.

Students will be able to recognize accurate statements about the mathematical processes embedded in word problems.

C. Students will be able to combine simple, compound, and compound-complex sentences fluently.

Students will be able to write a simple sentence with a subject and a predicate.

Students will be able to write compound-complex sentences in isolation.

D. Students will be able to make simple measurements in standard units.

Students will be able to convert between standard and nonstandard unit measurements.

Students will be able to make simple conversions within standard or nonstandard unit measurements.

E. Students will be able to discuss the key aspects of Roosevelt's foreign policy during World War II.

Students will be able to recognize accurate statements about Roosevelt's foreign policy during World War II.

Students will be able to compare the successes and failures of different presidents' foreign policies during times of conflict.

Exercise 4.2

Designing a Scale

Using the following form, design a scale for a recent goal you have addressed in class by filling in the score 4.0, 3.0, and 2.0 content.

Score 4.0	The student: • No major errors or omissions regarding the score 4.0 content
Score 3.5	In addition to score 3.0 performance, partial success at score 4.0 content
Score 3.0	The student: • No major errors or omissions regarding the score 3.0 content
Score 2.5	No major errors or omissions regarding score 2.0 content, and partial success at score 3.0 content
Score 2.0	The student: • No major errors or omissions regarding the score 2.0 content
Score 1.5	Partial success at score 2.0 content, but major errors or omissions regarding score 3.0 content
Score 1.0	With help, partial success at score 2.0 content and score 3.0 content
Score 0.5	With help, partial success at score 2.0 content, but not at score 3.0 content
Score 0.0	Even with help, no success

Exercise 4.3

Designing Noncognitive Scales

For each of the following scales, a noncognitive learning goal appears at the 3.0 score. Fill in the score 4.0 and 2.0 content.

1.

Score 4.0	The student:
	•
	No major errors or omissions regarding the score 4.0 content
Score 3.5	In addition to score 3.0 performance, partial success at score 4.0 content
Score 3.0	The student:
	• Discusses the consequences for breaking home and classroom rules.
	No major errors or omissions regarding the score 3.0 content
Score 2.5	No major errors or omissions regarding score 2.0 content, and partial success at score 3.0 content
Score 2.0	The student:
	•
	No major errors or omissions regarding the score 2.0 content
Score 1.5	Partial success at score 2.0 content, but major errors or omissions regarding score 3.0 content
Score 1.0	With help, partial success at score 2.0 content and score 3.0 content
Score 0.5	With help, partial success at score 2.0 content, but not at score 3.0 content
Score 0.0	Even with help, no success

1 of 2

2.

Score 4.0	The student: • **No major errors or omissions regarding the score 4.0 content**
Score 3.5	In addition to score 3.0 performance, partial success at score 4.0 content
Score 3.0	The student: • Picks up on and utilizes appropriate nonverbal language. **No major errors or omissions regarding the score 3.0 content**
Score 2.5	No major errors or omissions regarding score 2.0 content, and partial success at score 3.0 content
Score 2.0	The student: • **No major errors or omissions regarding the score 2.0 content**
Score 1.5	Partial success at score 2.0 content, but major errors or omissions regarding score 3.0 content
Score 1.0	**With help, partial success at score 2.0 content and score 3.0 content**
Score 0.5	With help, partial success at score 2.0 content, but not at score 3.0 content
Score 0.0	**Even with help, no success**

3.

Score 4.0	The student: • **No major errors or omissions regarding the score 4.0 content**
Score 3.5	In addition to score 3.0 performance, partial success at score 4.0 content
Score 3.0	The student: • Includes others in class assignments or games. **No major errors or omissions regarding the score 3.0 content**
Score 2.5	No major errors or omissions regarding score 2.0 content, and partial success at score 3.0 content
Score 2.0	The student: • **No major errors or omissions regarding the score 2.0 content**
Score 1.5	Partial success at score 2.0 content, but major errors or omissions regarding score 3.0 content
Score 1.0	**With help, partial success at score 2.0 content and score 3.0 content**
Score 0.5	With help, partial success at score 2.0 content, but not at score 3.0 content
Score 0.0	**Even with help, no success**

Designing and Teaching Learning Goals and Objectives • © 2009 Marzano Research Laboratory • marzanoresearch.com
Visit **marzanoresearch.com/classroomstrategies** to download this page.

Chapter 5

TEACHING IN A SYSTEM OF LEARNING GOALS

If teachers follow the direction provided in the previous four chapters, they will have a well-articulated system of learning goals as well as assessment tasks that go with these learning goals. As you have seen, learning goals can be organized into scales that help differentiate between levels of competence. This allows for a very powerful approach to instruction and assessment that employs options that are not available in the absence of a system of learning goals. In this chapter we consider two views of this new approach: one from the perspective of an entire year, the other from the perspective of a specific unit of instruction. We consider the year-long perspective first.

Learning Goals Over the Course of a Year

The curriculum over the course of a year is composed of individual units of instruction. Within a single unit of instruction a teacher typically addresses a few academic learning goals and even fewer noncognitive goals. Exactly how many goals should be identified is indeterminate. That noted, it makes some intuitive sense that a two-week unit of instruction can address somewhere between two and three goals without taxing the resources of individual teachers and the capacities of students. Thus, on average, a unit of instruction could handle 2.5 learning goals. If one extends this thinking, the entire year can address some 45 learning goals because the school year is typically thirty-six weeks long. If units are two weeks long, then 18 units will be executed during a year—each with 2 to 3 learning goals.

The 45 learning goals addressed throughout a year do not have to be 45 separate goals. Some learning goals might be addressed systematically during multiple units throughout the entire year. Others might be addressed during one unit only. To illustrate, consider table 5.1 (pages 80–81). It contains 31 sample learning goals that might be addressed by a middle school science teacher. It is important to note that table 5.1 reports only the target goals (score 3.0 content on the scale). For each of the goals, a scale like those depicted in chapter 4 would be constructed along with assessment tasks for each learning goal at score values 4.0, 3.0, and 2.0.

In all, table 5.1 lists 31 academic goals that are organized into 12 reporting topics. Those reporting topics are organized into four larger categories sometimes referred to as *strands*. From the preceding discussion, you can see that over the course of a year a teacher can probably accommodate about 45 learning goals—and maybe more. Taken at face value, this implies that there is room for 14 more goals.

Table 5.1 Middle School Science Goals Addressed in a Single Year

Strand #1: Earth and Space Sciences

Reporting Topic #1: Atmospheric Processes and the Water Cycle

Goal 1:   Students will illustrate how climate patterns are affected by the water cycle and its processes.

Goal 2:   Students will model how all levels of the earth's atmosphere (troposphere, stratosphere, mesosphere, and thermosphere) are affected by temperature and pressure.

Reporting Topic #2: Composition and Structure of the Earth

Goal 3:   Students will describe the unique composition of each of the earth's layers and how the earth is affected by the interaction of those layers.

Goal 4:   Students will describe the constructive and destructive forces that create and shape landforms.

Goal 5:   Students will illustrate each stage of the rock cycle (transitions to igneous, metamorphic, and sedimentary rock).

Reporting Topic #3: Composition and Structure of the Universe and the Earth's Place in It

Goal 6:   Students will find errors in explanations of how phenomena such as the day, the year, the moon phases, solar and lunar eclipses, tides, and shadows are created and changed by the orbits of the earth and the moon.

Goal 7:   Students will list the defining characteristics of each planet in the solar system and make basic comparisons between them.

Goal 8:   Students will model how the sun and the planets in our solar system interact.

Goal 9:   Students will explain the unique nature and defining elements of different celestial objects.

Strand #2: Life Sciences

Reporting Topic #4: Principles of Heredity and Related Concepts

Goal 10:   Students will classify specific reproductive characteristics (physical processes, heritable traits, and mutation risks) as either sexual or asexual.

Goal 11:   Students will illustrate different ways organisms can be affected by heritable traits (diseases, inherited physical abilities, and appearances).

Reporting Topic #5: Structure and Function of Cells and Organisms

Goal 12:   Students will match specific processes of cell division and differentiation to the correct prokaryotic or eukaryotic organism.

Goal 13:   Students will classify cells according to purpose in given multicellular organisms.

Goal 14:   Students will describe how cells, tissues, organs, and organ systems create interactive levels of organization.

Reporting Topic #6: Relationships Between Organisms and Their Physical Environment

Goal 15:   Students will describe the cause-and-effect relationships between humans and ecosystems.

Goal 16:   Students will explain how food chains and webs work and their places in an ecosystem.

Goal 17:   Students will illustrate how ecosystems transform matter in cycles.

Reporting Topic #7: Biological Evolution and the Diversity of Life

Goal 18:   Students will describe the key components of different theories on how life is thought to have begun and the different implications of those theories on current events and daily life.

Goal 19:   Students will explain how natural selection promotes unity and how it promotes diversity.

Strand #3: Physical Sciences

Reporting Topic #8: Structure and Properties of Matter

Goal 20: Students will describe the unique elements of isolated, closed, and open thermodynamic systems and make basic comparisons between them.

Goal 21: Students will describe the characteristics of different states of matter.

Goal 22: When given the composition, atomic number, melting point, and boiling point of an element, the student will name and classify it.

Reporting Topic #9: Sources and Properties of Energy

Goal 23: Students will classify a given energy as gravitational, chemical, mechanical, or nuclear.

Goal 24: Students will find errors in statements about the defining characteristics of motion, radiant, thermal, and motion energies and sound.

Goal 25: Students will describe the defining characteristics of geothermal, hydropower, wind, solar, ocean, and hydrogen energies and what makes them renewable.

Reporting Topic #10: Forces and Motion

Goal 26: Students will explain how factors such as force and friction can affect the motion of an object.

Goal 27: Students will describe the relationship between electricity and magnetism.

Goal 28: Students will explain how mass and distance affect gravitational force.

Strand #4: Nature of Science

Reporting Topic #11: Nature of Scientific Inquiry

Goal 29: Students will design and conduct multiple experiments that focus on replication.

Reporting Topic #12: Scientific Enterprise

Goal 30: Students will match specific scientific advancements with the scientist who made the discovery.

Goal 31: Students will explain how the scientific enterprise can raise ethical issues, and understand what those issues are.

However, that would make sense only if each of the learning goals were addressed in one unit only throughout the year. As mentioned previously, there are some goals that a teacher will want to address in more than one unit. To illustrate, consider the learning goal involving the nature of scientific inquiry (goal 29). It addresses designing and carrying out scientific experiments. A science teacher might want to include this in many, if not most, units of instruction throughout the year. Given that the teacher has room for 14 more learning goals (assuming that 45 can be addressed during a single school year), the teacher could include this goal in multiple units. To illustrate, consider table 5.2 (page 82), which contains a hypothetical arrangement of 12 units throughout the year and the learning goals that might be addressed in each of them.

As depicted in table 5.2, the teacher has organized the year into 12 units—roughly one for each of the reporting topics. (Of course, there are many ways to organize the goals shown in table 5.1. This relatively simplistic approach is offered for ease of discussion.) Note that goal 29, involving the scientific process, is addressed in the majority of units throughout the year. Thus, depending on how a teacher organizes his or her goals into units and how much time is devoted to those units, some goals may be repeated from unit to unit because of their importance and the developmental stages students go through as they learn them.

Table 5.2 Units and Learning Goals Throughout the Year

Unit #1: Atmospheric Processes and the Water Cycle	Length: 2 weeks Goals Addressed: 1, 2
Unit #2: Composition and Structure of the Earth	Length: 3 weeks Goals Addressed: 3, 4, 5, 29
Unit #3: Composition and Structure of the Universe	Length: 4 weeks Goals Addressed: 6, 7, 8, 9
Unit #4: Principles of Heredity and Related Concepts	Length: 3 weeks Goals Addressed: 10, 11, 29
Unit #5: Structure and Function of Cells and Organisms	Length: 4 weeks Goals Addressed: 12, 13, 14, 29
Unit #6: Relationships Between Organisms and Their Physical Environment	Length: 2 weeks Goals Addressed: 15, 16, 17
Unit #7: Biological Evolution and the Diversity of Life	Length: 3 weeks Goals Addressed: 18, 19, 29
Unit #8: Structure and Properties of Matter	Length: 3 weeks Goals Addressed: 20, 21, 22
Unit #9: Sources and Properties of Energy	Length: 3 weeks Goals Addressed: 23, 24, 25
Unit #10: Forces and Motion	Length: 5 weeks Goals Addressed: 26, 27, 28, 29
Unit #11: The Scientific Enterprise	Length: 2 weeks Goals Addressed: 29, 30
Unit #12: Your Future and Science	Length: 2 weeks Goals Addressed: 29, 30, 31

What About the Noncognitive Goals?

Noncognitive goals also have a place in the design of learning goals over the course of the year. For example, assume that a teacher identifies noncognitive learning goals for the areas of goal setting, emotional awareness, and working as a team member. These goals would be integrated into the planning for the year. For example, during the first unit, the teacher might address the noncognitive goal regarding working as a team member. He or she might elect to do so because it is a foundational skill for a classroom that will involve cooperative learning. During the next unit, the teacher might introduce the noncognitive goal regarding goal setting. During the third unit, the teacher would introduce the noncognitive goal regarding emotional awareness. Thus, quite early in the year, all three noncognitive goals would be introduced. These goals could then be revisited throughout the rest of the year without taking much instructional time away from the academic goals.

Learning Goals Within a Unit of Instruction

Within a unit of instruction, many elements of a classroom organized around a system of learning goals might appear quite traditional in nature. For example, the teacher will present experiences and information that will help students gain expertise in the goals for the unit. The teacher will also provide opportunities for students to review information that has been addressed previously. Likewise, the teacher will provide opportunities for students to practice skills and processes that have been addressed earlier. In short, an observer of a classroom that is organized around a system of learning goals might see many things that look identical to a classroom that is not organized around such a system; however, if that observer remained in the classroom for an extended period of time she would see some things that are not typically found in classrooms.

Students Gaining in Knowledge Throughout a Unit

One defining characteristic of a classroom organized around learning goals is that students progress in their competence throughout a unit of instruction and throughout the year for each learning goal. This is possible because the teacher has provided a scale for each learning goal that lends itself to tracking knowledge development. For example, consider the first unit of the year as depicted in table 5.2 (page 82). That unit addresses the following two learning goals from table 5.1 (pages 80–81):

> Goal 1: Students will illustrate how climate patterns are affected by the water cycle and its processes.

> Goal 2: Students will model how all levels of the earth's atmosphere (troposphere, stratosphere, mesosphere, and thermosphere) are affected by temperature and pressure.

As we saw in chapter 4, there will be a scale for each of these. To illustrate, table 5.3 depicts a scale for the first learning goal in the unit.

Table 5.3 Scale for the First Learning Goal in the First Unit

Score 4.0	The student: • Finds errors in illustrations depicting how a specific climate pattern is affected by the water cycle and its processes. **No major errors or omissions regarding the score 4.0 content**
Score 3.5	In addition to score 3.0 performance, partial success at score 4.0 content
Score 3.0	The student: • Illustrates how climate patterns are affected by the water cycle and its processes. **No major errors or omissions regarding the score 3.0 content**
Score 2.5	No major errors or omissions regarding score 2.0 content, and partial success at score 3.0 content

Score 2.0	The student:
	• Recognizes and recalls specific terminology, such as:
	  • Water cycle
	  • Climate/climate pattern
	• Recalls general information about the water cycle, such as:
	  • How it affects climate patterns
	No major errors or omissions regarding the score 2.0 content

Score 1.5	Partial success at score 2.0 content, and major errors or omissions regarding score 3.0 content
Score 1.0	With help, partial success at score 2.0 content and score 3.0 content
Score 0.5	With help, partial success at score 2.0 content, but not at score 3.0 content
Score 0.0	Even with help, no success

The teacher might begin the unit with a preassessment that addresses all of the content in the scale for each learning goal. The preassessment would be constructed using the assessment tasks associated with the score 4.0, 3.0, and 2.0 learning goals. Over the course of the unit and the year, the teacher would design other assessment tasks for score 4.0, 3.0, and 2.0.

Because the teacher has not provided any direct instruction relative to the content in these two goals at the beginning of the unit, students would typically receive low scores on each of the two scales for the preassessment. For example, one student might receive a preassessment score of 2.0 on the first learning goal and a score of 1.5 on the second learning goal. As the unit progresses, students would be provided with instructional activities that increase their competence in each learning goal. Thus, students' scores would improve as the unit progresses. To illustrate, consider figure 5.1 and figure 5.2 (page 86).

Figures 5.1 and 5.2 depict the progress of one student on two learning goals across the first unit of instruction. As shown previously, the student began with a score of 2.0 on the first goal, but increased (overall) to a score of 2.5 by the end of the unit. Likewise, the student began with a score of 1.0 on the second goal, but increased to a score of 3.0 by the end of the unit. Using line graphs like those shown in figure 5.1 and figure 5.2 (page 86), students can chart their own progress over time. Some teachers and students prefer to track progress using bar graphs, as shown in figure 5.3 (page 87) and figure 5.4 (page 88). (A reproducible master for a student progress chart is provided on page 94.)

In a classroom organized around learning goals, students can begin a unit with relatively low scores and still end the unit with high scores. As you will see, students can keep raising their scores on learning goals throughout the entire year. This is in contrast to a system in which low scores on assessments at the beginning of a unit or year penalize students throughout the entire unit or year. For example, if a student in a traditional classroom receives a low score on the very first test, he will have limited the highest score that he can receive at the end of the grading period because this low score is averaged with scores from the other assessments during the same grading period. In a classroom organized around learning goals, a score on a particular scale for a learning goal represents the student's status at one point in time only. At a later point in time, if the student demonstrates enhanced competence, his score changes to represent his new status.

Students Taking Responsibility for Demonstrating Competence

Another nontraditional aspect of a classroom organized around learning goals is that students can design their own ways to demonstrate progress on learning goals. It makes sense that at the beginning of the year, the teacher will be the one to design assessment tasks that illustrate progress in a specific learning goal. That is, at the beginning of the year, the teacher will present students with assessment tasks that illustrate a competence level of score 2.0, tasks that demonstrate a competence level of score 3.0, and tasks that demonstrate a competence level of score 4.0. As you saw in previous chapters, such tasks will be constructed as learning goals are being articulated. However, after students become familiar with the system, they can identify the types of tasks and activities they want to create in order to demonstrate competence at various levels. To illustrate, consider the student with the initial scores of 2.0 and 1.0 on learning goals 1 and 2, respectively, as depicted in figures 5.1 and 5.2 (page 86). After examining the scale for the first learning goal, the student might propose that to demonstrate score 3.0 competence, he will be prepared to answer specific questions from the back of the chapter in the textbook that addresses the topic. Another student with the same initial score might propose that she write a brief essay describing this content and present it to the teacher. Still a third student with an initial score of 2.0 might propose that she make an oral presentation regarding the score 3.0 content.

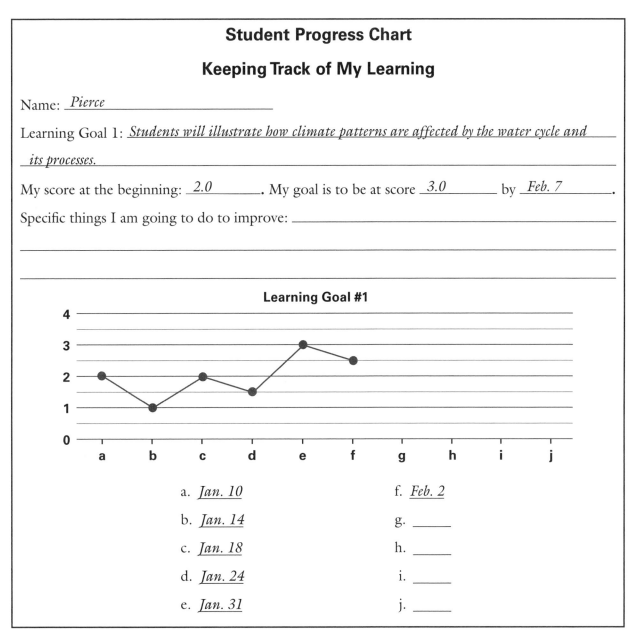

Student Progress Chart

Keeping Track of My Learning

Name: _Pierce_

Learning Goal 1: _Students will illustrate how climate patterns are affected by the water cycle and its processes._

My score at the beginning: _2.0_. My goal is to be at score _3.0_ by _Feb. 7_.

Specific things I am going to do to improve: _____

Learning Goal #1

a. _Jan. 10_   f. _Feb. 2_

b. _Jan. 14_   g. _____

c. _Jan. 18_   h. _____

d. _Jan. 24_   i. _____

e. _Jan. 31_   j. _____

Figure 5.1 Line graph depicting student growth for goal 1.

In a classroom organized around learning goals, then, students have the right and the invitation to take control of the manner in which they demonstrate competence at a specific score value for a specific scale. At any point in time, a student can approach the teacher and propose a way to increase his or her score on the scale for a particular learning goal.

Cooperative Learning Structures

In chapter 1, you saw that cooperative learning goals can have a potentially powerful effect on student learning. In the context of a classroom organized around learning goals, teachers can use cooperative structures as a resource to help students progress through the knowledge levels of a particular scale for a particular goal. Angela O'Donnell (2006) has identified a number of cooperative structures that could be particularly helpful to this end.

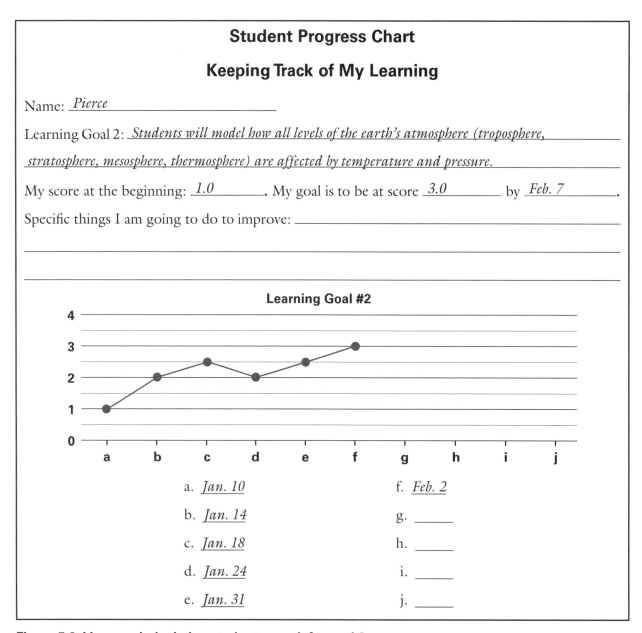

Student Progress Chart

Keeping Track of My Learning

Name: _Pierce_

Learning Goal 2: _Students will model how all levels of the earth's atmosphere (troposphere,_
stratosphere, mesosphere, thermosphere) are affected by temperature and pressure.

My score at the beginning: _1.0_ . My goal is to be at score _3.0_ by _Feb. 7_ .

Specific things I am going to do to improve: _____

_____

Learning Goal #2

a. _Jan. 10_   f. _Feb. 2_

b. _Jan. 14_   g. _____

c. _Jan. 18_   h. _____

d. _Jan. 24_   i. _____

e. _Jan. 31_   j. _____

Figure 5.2 Line graph depicting student growth for goal 2.

One of those structures is *group investigation*, in which students are organized into groups to investigate a specific topic (Sharan & Hertz-Lazarowitz, 1980). In the context of the discussion in this book, a topic would be a learning goal or a set of learning goals addressed during the unit of instruction. Team members in each cooperative group would gather information about content for various levels of the scale for each learning goal—the informational answers that would demonstrate competence for score 2.0, 3.0, and 4.0. Cooperative teams would be carefully structured so that all levels of expertise regarding the learning goals are represented in each team. That is, the teacher would try to ensure that each team has a student or students who are knowledgeable about the topic so they might provide assistance to the students who are less knowledgeable.

Class time would be scheduled so that students can meet in their teams frequently, if not on a daily basis. Although each student must independently demonstrate competence on the scale for each learn-

Student Progress Chart

Keeping Track of My Learning

Name: _Pierce_

Learning Goal 1: _Students will illustrate how climate patterns are affected by the water cycle and its processes._

My score at the beginning: _2.0_. My goal is to be at score _3.0_ by _Feb. 7_.

Specific things I am going to do to improve: _____

_____

_____

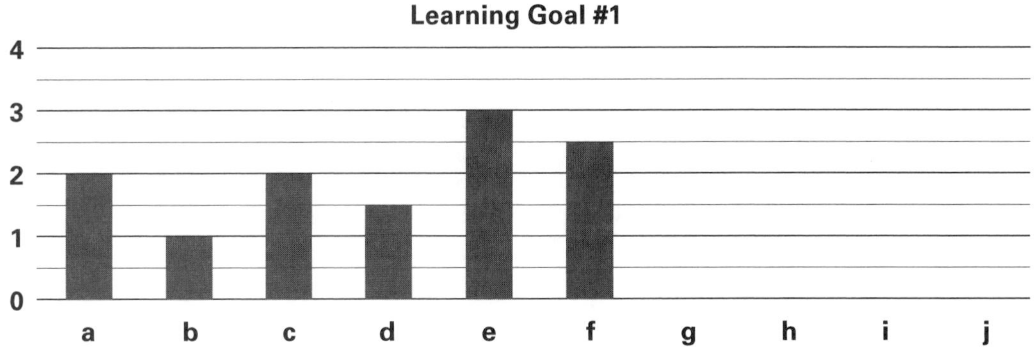

Learning Goal #1

a. _Jan. 10_   f. _Feb. 2_

b. _Jan. 14_   g. _____

c. _Jan. 18_   h. _____

d. _Jan. 24_   i. _____

e. _Jan. 31_   j. _____

Figure 5.3 Bar graph depicting student growth for goal 1.

ing goal, the cooperative group serves as a support group and informal tutorial group for students who are having difficulty working through the levels of knowledge of the scale for a particular learning goal.

A closely related cooperative structure is *jigsaw*, which was designed by Elliot Aronson and colleagues (1978). O'Donnell (2006) notes that it is one of the original cooperative learning techniques. She describes it in the following way:

> Students are assigned to four-person heterogeneous groups that are assigned topics on which they are to become experts. For example, if the group were learning about the rainforest, each member of the group would be responsible for becoming an expert on a subtopic (e.g., birds and animals of the rainforest, people who live in the rainforest, plants, and

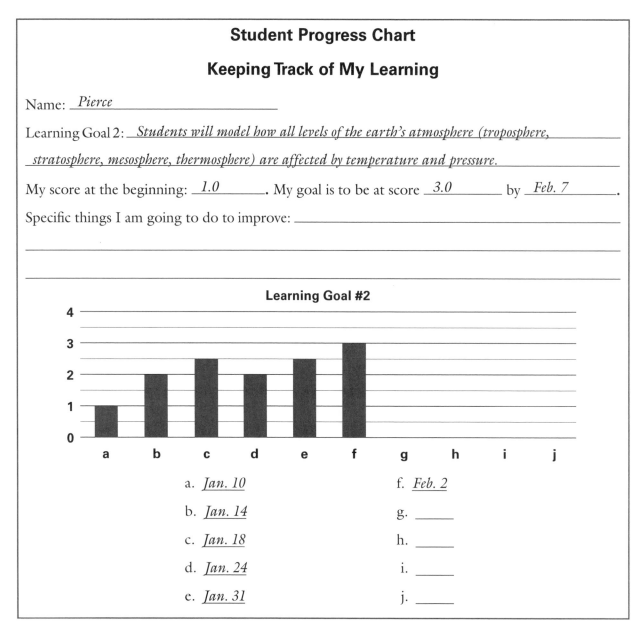

Figure 5.4 Bar graph depicting student growth for goal 2.

the destruction of the rainforest). Students with the same "expert topic" from different teams meet in groups to discuss their topic. Their task is to become as knowledgeable as possible about the topic. They then return to their groups and teach the material to other students in their groups. (p. 792)

Relative to the scale for a particular learning goal, expert groups would be assigned to the content for score 2.0, 3.0, and 4.0 for a given scale. Thus, there would be three expert groups for each scale. Each expert group is tasked with learning as much as possible about the content for a particular score value on the scale. Individuals in each expert group then go back to their cooperative groups and share the information.

Another cooperative structure that lends itself to a classroom organized around goals is *peer tutoring*. There are a number of models of peer tutoring (see O'Donnell, 2006 for a discussion of the various approaches), but the one that appears to apply best to the discussion in this chapter is *structured tutorial interaction* (King, Staffieri, & Adelgais, 1998). Within structured tutorial interaction, tutors are instructed to interact with a tutee using a specific sequence of activities. Specifically, tutors are taught to explain what they know about a particular topic, explain why they know the information is accurate, and then try to help their tutees make linkages to what they already know.

Results of studies on this approach indicate that it is particularly effective in developing an understanding of complex information that requires inferences and application. Thus, structured tutorial interaction would be particularly useful for score 3.0 and 4.0 content for many learning goals. Tutors should be volunteer students who have demonstrated score 3.0 or score 4.0 competence early in a unit. For example, some students might demonstrate score 3.0 or score 4.0 competence in the learning goals for a unit at the very outset. These students can act as peer tutors for those students who are having difficulty with specific learning goals. As described in the next section, over the course of the year, more and more students will demonstrate score 3.0 or 4.0 competence for learning goals early in the sequence of instruction. Indeed, some students might complete the entire curriculum well before the year is over. These students can volunteer to be peer tutors or can work on advanced content.

Continuous Improvement in Learning

Perhaps the most powerful aspect of a classroom organized around learning goals is that students can move at their own pace. As described previously, after students have demonstrated score 3.0 or score 4.0 competence for the learning goals in a particular unit, they can volunteer to act as peer tutors for students who are having difficulty reaching that level within the time constraints of the unit. It is very important that peer tutoring be a volunteer activity.

Those students who do not elect to volunteer can begin working on other learning goals that will be addressed in subsequent units. For the most part, this would be done on an independent study basis. The teacher would provide resources and guidance for these "fast track" students, but the pace of their development would be left up to them. Students could elect to work on learning goals that will be the topic of the next unit or learning goals that will be the topic of units during the next quarter or even the next semester. If a student demonstrates score 3.0 or 4.0 competence on all the learning goals that form the curriculum for the entire year, he can begin addressing learning goals for the content at the next grade level.

Obviously, if an entire school is organized in this fashion, the transition to content that is at higher grade levels is made relatively easy. Descriptions of how such a schoolwide or districtwide system would operate are provided in *Classroom Assessment and Grading That Work* (Marzano, 2006) and in *Formative Assessment and Standards-Based Grading* (Marzano, in press). However, even if a teacher is the only one in her school who organizes her classroom around learning goals, accommodating students who demonstrate competence in grade-level learning goals early in the year simply requires her to consult the curriculum for the next year.

If a teacher operates in a self-contained classroom where he is responsible for (let's say) language arts, mathematics, science, and social studies, then a student who demonstrated score 3.0 or 4.0 competence in all learning goals for one subject area (mathematics, for example) can begin working on learning goals for another subject area in which he is not ahead of the classroom pace (language arts, for example). If a student completes all learning goals for all four subject areas, he begins working on goals at the next grade level and/or volunteers as a peer tutor.

A classroom organized around learning goals is also beneficial for students who do not demonstrate score 3.0 or 4.0 competence within the time allocated for a unit of instruction. For example, assume that after the first unit of instruction that addresses two learning goals, a particular student has demonstrated score 1.0 and 2.0 competence on the two goals, respectively. While every effort would be made to ensure that all students reach at least score 3.0 competence before the beginning of the next unit, it is probably inevitable that some students will simply not be ready by the time the unit ends. The next unit of instruction addresses two different learning goals. The students who have not demonstrated at least score 3.0 competence still participate in the new unit and the new learning goals. However, these students would have access to tutorial help during the second unit (and the third unit, and so on) for any of the learning goals previously addressed. As described earlier, this tutorial help can come from volunteer students who have demonstrated competence early. Ideally, a teacher will also have access to adult help for students who begin lagging behind systematically on learning goals. This help can come (other than from the teacher) in the form of teacher aids, paraprofessionals, and after-school tutorials. Obviously, if an entire school is organized around learning goals, such help can be built into resource allocations. If a teacher does not have the help of an aid or paraprofessional, then he provides as much help for students as is available through peer tutorials.

One important aspect of a classroom organized around learning goals is that students should be allowed the entire year to demonstrate score 3.0 or 4.0 competence for learning goals. That is, at any time during the year, a student can raise a scale score on any of the learning goals addressed throughout the year. For example, a student entering the fourth quarter of the academic year might have scores of 2.0 or less on 10 of the 31 learning goals addressed throughout the year (see table 5.1, pages 80–81). During that last quarter, the student could raise the scores on these 10 learning goals. In short, at any time throughout the academic year, any student can revisit past learning goals and demonstrate advanced competence.

The Issue of Grading

It is probably safe to say that most teachers currently operate within a system that requires some form of an overall grade at the end of specific grading periods. How does a classroom organized around learning goals address traditional grades? This issue is addressed in depth in the book *Formative Assessment and Standards-Based Grading: The Classroom Strategies Series* (Marzano, in press). We address it here briefly.

Ideally, overall or "omnibus" grades would not be assigned in a system organized around learning goals, but they can be if a teacher, school, or district so desires. To do so, a teacher would simply average the final scores on each learning goal addressed during that grading period and translate that average scale score to a traditional letter grade. For example, assume that 10 learning goals had been addressed during the first quarter. Also assume that a particular student received the following scores on those 10 learning goals:

Goal 1: 2.0

Goal 2: 2.5

Goal 3: 3.0

Goal 4: 2.0

Goal 5: 3.0

Goal 6: 2.5

Goal 7: 1.5

Goal 8: 2.0

Goal 9: 2.0

Goal 10: 3.0

The average of these scores is 2.35. This could be translated into an overall grade using a scale like that in table 5.4.

Table 5.4 Conversion Scale to Traditional Grades

Average Scale Score		Traditional Grade	Average Scale Score		Traditional Grade
3.51–4.00		A	2.17–2.33		C
3.00–3.50		A-	2.00–2.16		C-
2.84–2.99		B+	1.84–1.99		D+
2.67–2.83		B	1.67–1.83		D
2.50–2.66		B-	1.50–1.66		D-
2.34–2.49		C+	.00–1.49		F

In this case, the student would receive a grade of C+.

Let's assume that during the next quarter, 10 more learning goals were addressed. The teacher would average the final scores on these topics *along with* the final scores on the topics addressed during the first quarter to obtain a cumulative average for all topics addressed over the semester. It is important to remember that during the semester, the student would have had the opportunity to raise scores on learning goals addressed during the first quarter. Thus, the scores from the first quarter for a specific student might have changed as follows:

Goal 1: Increased from 2.0 to 3.0

Goal 2: Increased from 2.5 to 3.0

Goal 3: Stayed the same at 3.0

Goal 4: Increased from 2.0 to 3.0

Goal 5: Increased from 3.0 to 4.0

Goal 6: Increased from 2.5 to 3.0

Goal 7: Increased from 1.5 to 2.0

Goal 8: Increased from 2.0 to 3.0

Goal 9: Increased from 2.0 to 2.5

Goal 10: Stayed the same at 3.0

The scores for this student on the learning goals addressed during the second quarter might be:

Goal 11: 2.5

Goal 12: 2.0

Goal 13: 2.0

Goal 14: 3.0

Goal 15: 2.5

Goal 16: 3.0

Goal 17: 2.0

Goal 18: 1.5

Goal 19: 3.0

Goal 20: 2.0

The average final score for these 20 learning goals (the final score for the goals introduced in the first quarter and the most current scores for goals introduced in the second quarter) is 2.65, which translates to a grade of B-.

After the third quarter, the teacher would average the final scores on all topics addressed during that quarter and the previous two to create an overall grade, and so on. Thus the grade at the end of each quarter and the end of the year represents the student's *cumulative* learning on all learning goals addressed up to that point in time. This system encourages students to keep increasing their learning on all the relevant content throughout the course of the year and rewards their efforts to continually develop their knowledge.

This system is quite different from one that does not allow students to demonstrate increased competence in content that has been previously taught. For example, a grading system that does not allow students to demonstrate that they have increased their knowledge of first-quarter content during the second quarter (or later in the year) fails to acknowledge that students might now understand content they previously did not understand. Such a system is not in keeping with the spirit of most state standards documents. Specifically, most state standards documents identify content that should be learned *by the end of the school year*. It is thus implicit in most state standards documents that students should have opportunities to raise their scores on content that has been addressed previously in the year.

Summary

Once learning goals have been designed and differentiated, teachers must be able to implement them effectively over the course of a unit and the course of a year. By organizing the learning goals into reporting topics, teachers can easily design units around a reasonable number of related goals. Noncognitive goals can be woven in as well, without taking away from instruction. This kind of organization ensures all goals are being addressed as often as necessary throughout the course of an entire school year. Within a unit, this system encourages cooperative learning (through peer tutoring) and allows students to keep track of their own scores. Because students are explicitly aware of their strengths and weaknesses, they can take more responsibility and make independent efforts toward demonstrating competency and raising scores. As the school year progresses, students can raise their scores on any learning goal at any time and are thus not penalized for initial misunderstandings or a slow start. By implementing a system of clear and well-organized learning goals, students can truly be held accountable for their own continuous learning throughout the course of a year.

Student Progress Chart

Keeping Track of My Learning

Name: _____

Learning Goal: _____

_____

My score at the beginning: _____. My goal is to be at score _____ by _____.

Specific things I am going to do to improve: _____

_____

_____

Learning Goal: _____

	a	b	c	d	e	f	g	h	i	j
4										
3										
2										
1										
0										

a. _____   f. _____

b. _____   g. _____

c. _____   h. _____

d. _____   i. _____

e. _____   j. _____

EPILOGUE

The system described in this book, when embraced fully by an individual teacher, has some very powerful implications for classroom instruction. As you have seen, a classroom organized around learning goals provides students with clear targets for their learning and scales that articulate the simpler content and the more complex content for each learning goal. Additionally, such a classroom uses cooperative structures to establish an environment in which students are resource providers and tutors for one another, and it does not penalize students for initial confusion or a slow start. Finally, a classroom organized around learning goals puts no limits on what a student can accomplish in a given year. Any student can move as rapidly as he or she wishes through the curriculum for a given year and even beyond if he or she so desires. By carefully tailoring learning goals and teaching them in a system that encourages pacing flexibility and student empowerment, teachers can get an accurate and complete picture of each student's improvement and proficiency as well as the improvement and proficiency of the entire class. Armed with such knowledge, teachers will be well prepared to help students raise their achievement.

APPENDIX A

ANSWERS TO EXERCISES

Answers to Exercise 2.1

Learning Goals vs. Activities and Assignments

1. *Students will be able to recognize the protagonist, theme, and voice of a piece of literature.*

   This is a learning goal. There is a desired outcome specified (recognizing the protagonist, theme, and voice of a piece of literature).

2. *Students will produce a book report on a book of their choice, including a table of contents, with proper pagination and format throughout.*

   This is primarily an activity. The cognitive or behavioral outcome is not clearly specified. There is no particular level of understanding or ability that is needed to produce a book report with these specifications. There are no clear standards for judging the quality of the product.

3. *Given a set of coordinates, students will be able to graph the slope of a line.*

   This is a learning goal. There are clearly defined cognitive and psychomotor skills that students must demonstrate.

4. *Students will compare and describe the slopes of two lines.*

   This is an activity. Students are asked to engage in a complex cognitive behavior—comparing—but there is no explicit expectation as to what students should understand better or be able to do better.

5. *Students will understand the differences and similarities between metamorphic, igneous, and sedimentary rock.*

   This is a learning goal. Unlike statement 4, which also involves a comparison, there is a clear outcome regarding student understanding.

6. *Students will understand how the Borgia family influenced the Renaissance.*

   This is a learning goal. There is a clear outcome regarding what students will understand.

7. *Students will be able to explain how the problems created by the French and Indian War contributed to causes of the American Revolution.*

   This is a learning goal. There is a clear desired outcome regarding the understanding of a causal relationship.

8. *Students will produce a play dramatizing the problems created by the French and Indian War and how they contributed to causes of the American Revolution.*

   This is a learning goal. There's a clear desired outcome regarding the understanding of a causal relationship.

9. *Students will understand that matter is made up of atoms and that atoms, in turn, are made up of subatomic particles.*

   This is a learning goal. There is a clear outcome regarding what students should know about atoms.

10. *Students will write a paper describing the relationships among atoms and subatomic particles.*

    This is an activity. The statement calls for something to be done (a paper to be written) and specifies a topic (the relationships among atoms and subatomic particles) but does not make clear the desired outcome regarding student understanding or skill.

Answers to Exercise 2.2

Declarative vs. Procedural Knowledge

1. *Creating a line graph to represent data*

   This statement is procedural. There is a certain amount of declarative information required (students must be familiar with data sets and line graphs), but the emphasis is on the creation of a line graph that accurately reflects a set of data. The teacher is asking the student to *do* something.

2. *Describing the events that led to the Cold War*

   This statement is declarative. Students are required to demonstrate knowledge of the Cold War. Again, a certain amount of procedural knowledge is required in that students must describe what they know, but the emphasis is clearly on knowledge of the Cold War and not on speaking or describing.

3. *Determining breathing rate and heart rate*

   Given the way this statement is worded, it could be either procedural or declarative. If the emphasis is on information about breathing and heart rate (what rates are common in resting, normal, and active states, for example), the statement would be declarative. In that case, it might be reworded into something like the following: *Students will understand the common breathing and heart rates for resting, normal, and active states for people their own age.* If the focus is on the process of finding these rates, the statement would be procedural. In that case, it might be reworded to reflect a statement like the following: *Students will be able to find and calculate the breathing and heart rates for themselves and others.*

4. *Refusal skills*

   This statement could be either declarative or procedural. If the focus is only on having an understanding of refusal skills and the situations in which they might be useful, the focus is on declarative information, and the statement can be reworded to read as follows: *Students will understand proper refusal skills and the academic and social situations in which they would be used.* If the teacher wants the students to put this knowledge to use, the focus would be primarily procedural. It could be reworded like this: *Students will be able to demonstrate proper refusal skills in appropriate academic and social situations.*

5. *Characteristics of chance events*

   This statement is declarative. Students are required to understand the defining characteristics of a concept—chance events.

6. *Keyboarding techniques*

   This statement could be either declarative or procedural. If the emphasis is on the physical process of keyboarding, it would be procedural knowledge; if the emphasis is on understanding the position of the keys, it would be declarative knowledge.

7. *Keeping in rhythm*

   This statement is primarily procedural. It could be argued that if the emphasis is on understanding how to keep rhythm then it could be declarative as well, but most often people do not understand rhythm in an informational way. We understand rhythm by the process of keeping it.

8. *The relationship between the seasons and the tilt of the earth*

   This statement is declarative. It requires an understanding of causal relationships.

9. *Survey sampling technique*

   This statement could be either declarative or procedural. It is most likely that the intended focus is on the use of survey sampling techniques for a given purpose, and in that case, the statement would be procedural and could read something like: *Students will be able to use appropriate survey sampling techniques and report results.*

10. *Front-end rounding*

    This statement could be either declarative or procedural. It is likely that the teacher would want students not only to have declarative knowledge of front-end rounding (how it is done and what its purpose is), but to be able to perform the process as well. If the teacher's aim is the former, the statement might read as follows: *Students will understand the purpose and steps in front-end rounding.* If the teacher's aim is the latter, the statement will read like this: *Students will be able to use front-end rounding.*

Answers to Exercise 2.3

Translating General Statements Into Learning Goals

1. *Language arts general statement: Speaking effectively*

   Goal statement: Students will be able to present a five- to seven-minute oral argument on the topic of their choosing. The argument will have a clear introduction, main premise, supporting statements, and conclusion. Students will verbally acknowledge correct grammar throughout.

2. *Mathematics general statement: Reducing fractions*

   Goal statement: Students will be able to recognize complex fractions that can be reduced to simpler terms and will be able to perform the arithmetic necessary to correctly complete the reduction.

3. *Science general statement: Understanding photosynthesis*

   Goal statement: Students will be able to describe how photosynthesis functions in terms of plant respiration, nutrition, and growth, and will be able to identify factors that support or inhibit photosynthesis.

4. *Social studies general statement: Knowing local history*

   Goal statement: Students will be able to list five important events in local history and explain why each of them is significant.

5. *Physical education general statement: Agility*

   Goal statement: Students will be able to catch a ball thrown to their left or right sides.

6. *Technology general statement: Using Excel*

   Goal statement: Students will be able to enter data into an Excel spreadsheet, apply variable and value labels to the data, and perform simple descriptive data analysis such as calculating means, standard deviations, and percentages.

7. *World languages general statement: Spanish conversation*

   Goal statement: Students will be able to converse with one another in Spanish about the type of food they like for breakfast.

8. *The arts general statement: Music appreciation*

   Goal statement: Students will be able to identify their favorite type of music and explain in specific terms why that type is their favorite.

9. *Language arts general statement: Reading comprehension*

   Goal statement: Students will be able to discuss explicitly and implicitly stated themes and ideas.

10. *Mathematics general statement: Estimating*

Goal statement: Students will be able to estimate sums and differences mentally.

Answers to Exercise 2.4

Designing Assessment Tasks for Learning Goals

1. *Students will be able to use knowledge of prefixes, suffixes, and roots to spell words.*

   Sample assessment: Use the provided lists of prefixes, suffixes, and roots to assemble a word.

2. *Students will explain the rules and strategies of a team game.*

   Sample assessment: We have been studying the sport of basketball. Following is a set of statements about the rules of the game. Identify each statement as either true or false. The last question outlines a specific scenario common to the sport. Outline the strategy you would use in that situation to win the game.

3. *Students will explain how an organism's behavior is related to the physical characteristics of its environment.*

   Sample assessment: We have been studying the Arctic and Antarctic climates and the animals that live there. Provide a brief description of the climate, and then choose your favorite of the animals we have studied. How does this animal get its food, and how is this related to the environment in which it lives?

4. *Students will illustrate how food works as an energy source.*

   Sample assessment: Using the diagram of the human body provided, create a flowchart illustrating how food is digested and used as energy.

5. *Students will be able to create and separate a simple mixture such as salt and sand.*

   Sample assessment: Use the container provided to mix two of the substances in front of you. Keep in mind when making your mixture that you will also have to separate the substances back into pure form.

6. *Students will be able to analyze a speaker's presentation with an eye for logical fallacy.*

   Sample assessment: We will be giving class presentations in the next few days. When another student is speaking, take notes on his or her main points in the order of presentation. When the speech is finished, you will have a few moments to look over your notes and write a brief review of the speech. Please include your thoughts on the logic of the argument presented and why it did or did not convince you.

7. *Students will describe the articles and amendments of the Constitution of the United States.*

Sample assessment: We have been studying the articles and amendments of the Constitution of the United States. Choose an article or amendment you consider to be important in today's society and write a brief description of what you think would change if that article or amendment had never been drafted.

8. *Students will be able to determine cause and effect of historical events in the exploration of the Americas.*

   Sample assessment: We have been studying the discovery and exploration of the Americas. Provide a brief description of the lives and cultures of people native to the United States and what happened to these people as a result of the age of European exploration. Name two specific events, and explain why they exemplify the cause-and-effect relationship of the Native Americans to the European explorers and pilgrims.

9. *Students will be able to generate a hypothesis or a prediction based on an observation.*

   Sample assessment: Today we will watch four chemical reactions involving three chemicals. Write down what you see as we go along. At the end of class, I will give you the names of two chemicals. Think about these chemicals and how they are different from and similar to the chemicals we saw in reactions during class. Make a prediction about how these two chemicals will react, and explain your reasoning.

10. *Students will determine the main idea and supporting details of an expository text.*

    Sample assessment: Read the following excerpt. Write a few sentences describing what the main idea is, and name at least two supporting details you found in the text.

Answers to Exercise 3.1

Identifying Different Types of Retrieval Goals

1. *Students will be able to identify from a list the steps involved in photosynthesis.*

   This statement is an example of recognition. Students are asked to identify correct information when it is presented; they do not need to produce the information themselves. Rather, they will react to the information presented to them.

2. *Students will be able to play a piece of music.*

   This statement is an example of execution. Playing a piece of music requires students to demonstrate a particular set of movements to accomplish a task.

3. *Students will be able to name six prominent world political leaders.*

   This statement is an example of recall. Students are asked to retrieve previously presented information and replicate it accurately.

4. *Students will be able to list the continents.*

   This statement is an example of recall. Students are asked to retrieve previously presented information and replicate it accurately.

5. *Students will be able to identify accurate versus inaccurate information about presidential candidates.*

   This statement is an example of recognition. Students are asked to distinguish between accurate and inaccurate information; they do not need to produce the information themselves, but they are required to react to the information presented to them.

6. *Students will be able to list the major combatant nations of World War II.*

   This statement is an example of recall. Students are asked to retrieve previously presented information and replicate it accurately.

7. *Students will be able to select mammals from a list of animals.*

   This statement is an example of recognition. Students are asked to identify correct types of information when presented with a larger list; they do not need to produce the information themselves, but they do need to react to the information presented to them.

8. *Students will be able to identify examples of complete sentences.*

   This statement is an example of recognition. Students are asked to identify correct types of information when presented with a larger list; they do not need to produce the information themselves, but they do need to react to the information presented to them.

9. *Students will be able to list examples of proper nouns.*

   This statement is an example of recall. Students are asked to retrieve previously presented information and replicate it accurately.

10. *Students will be able to perform addition using two-digit numbers.*

   This statement is an example of execution. Complex addition requires students to demonstrate a particular set of procedures to accomplish the larger task.

Designing and Teaching Learning Goals and Objectives • © 2009 Marzano Research Laboratory • marzanoresearch.com
Visit **marzanoresearch.com/classroomstrategies** to download this page.

Answers to Exercise 3.2

Identifying Different Types of Comprehension Goals

1. *Students will be able to describe the major components of an organism's behavior cycle.*

   This statement is an example of integrating. Students must understand the major components of an organism's behavior cycle and how that cycle works.

2. *Students will be able to create a flowchart that shows the steps involved in tying a shoe.*

   This statement is an example of symbolizing. The student must translate knowledge about the steps involved in tying a shoe into an abstract form. Whether the students fill in the flowchart using linguistic descriptions or illustrations, they are using symbolization.

3. *Students will be able to describe the key reasons why eating healthy food provides the body with more energy.*

   This statement is an example of integrating. Students must identify the defining characteristics of the generalization that people who eat healthy food live longer than people who do not.

4. *Students will be able to describe the major contributions to society made by Dr. Martin Luther King, Jr.*

   This statement is an example of integrating. Students must take what they know about Dr. Martin Luther King, Jr., and identify the major contributions of his life.

5. *Students will be able to summarize the results of a scientific experiment.*

   This statement is an example of integrating. By nature, a summary requires students to distinguish between important and unimportant information. In this case, they must look at all of the results of an experiment and select the most important in order to provide a summary.

6. *Students will be able to diagram the transitions between key ideas in an expository text.*

   This statement is an example of symbolizing. The objective requires the students to create a diagram, which is an abstract representation of the transitions between important ideas.

7. *Students will be able to create pictorial representations of the cause-and-effect sequence of an event in history.*

   This statement is an example of symbolizing. This objective requires students to select which items or events fit into a specific cause-and-effect sequence, but given that they are required to use nonlinguistic representations in order to accomplish the task, symbolization is the major comprehension process they will employ.

8. *Students will be able to paraphrase the important points made by a speaker.*

This statement is an example of integrating. Like summarizing, paraphrasing by nature requires students to distinguish between key and supporting information.

9. *Students will be able to use manipulatives to demonstrate the process of multiplication.*

This statement is an example of symbolizing. When students use blocks or marbles (for example) to depict the steps in a process, they are creating an abstract representation.

10. *Students will be able to describe the defining aspects of a musical genre.*

This statement is an example of integrating. Students must have a deep enough understanding of a specific musical genre to describe its defining characteristics.

Designing and Teaching Learning Goals and Objectives • © 2009 Marzano Research Laboratory • marzanoresearch.com
Visit **marzanoresearch.com/classroomstrategies** to download this page.

Answers to Exercise 3.3

Identifying Different Types of Analysis Goals

1. *Students will be able to organize a group of sentences into the categories simple, compound, complex.*

   This is an example of classifying. Students are asked to organize sentences into superordinate categories.

2. *Given a group of statements, students will be able to generate conclusions that flow from them.*

   This is an example of generalizing. Students are asked to translate specific information to a more general form.

3. *Students will be able to compare and contrast classical, romantic, and modern styles of music.*

   This is an example of matching. Students are asked to examine similarities and differences between types of music.

4. *Students will be able to develop an office floor plan based on specific principles of communication and justify its layout.*

   This is an example of specifying. Students are asked to reason from a set of principles to create a floor plan that fills a specific need and then justify the plan according to those principles.

5. *Students will describe how their observations are similar or dissimilar to others' observations.*

   This is an example of matching. Students are asked to articulate similarities and differences.

6. *Students will be able to categorize types of statistical calculations according to their use.*

   This is an example of classifying. Students are asked to organize information according to superordinate categories.

7. *Students will be able to identify and correct logical errors in a written argument.*

   This is an example of analyzing errors. Students are asked to identify and correct errors.

8. *Students will be able to infer the global implications of a proposed energy technology.*

   This is an example of generalizing. Students are asked to take current information and speculate on its more general impact.

9. *Students will be able to judge what colors would best enhance a work space.*

   This is an example of specifying. Students are asked to articulate a set of specifics in response to a given need and explain their conclusions.

10. *Students will be able to identify problems in the flow of their writing and correct them.*

    This is an example of analyzing errors. Students are asked to identify and correct mistakes and problems in their work.

Designing and Teaching Learning Goals and Objectives • © 2009 Marzano Research Laboratory • marzanoresearch.com
Visit **marzanoresearch.com/classroomstrategies** to download this page.

Answers to Exercise 3.4

Identifying Different Types of Knowledge Utilization Goals

1. *Students will be able to select the best brushstroke for creating a composition that focuses on texture.*

   This statement is an example of decision making. Given the specific focus of texture, students must use what they know about brushstrokes to select the one that would be the most suitable for creating a composition that fulfills the obligation of the objective.

2. *Students will be able to design an alternative mode of transportation with attention to energy efficiency.*

   This statement is an example of problem solving. Students must design a mode of transportation under the constraint that it is energy efficient.

3. *Students will be able to discuss hypothetical conclusions to the Vietnam War if President Kennedy had not been assassinated.*

   This statement is an example of investigating. Students are asked to dissect a particular time period and, based on facts, speculations, and opinions of others, come to a hypothetical conclusion.

4. *Students will be able to generate and test ideas about how to win a tennis game.*

   This statement is an example of experimenting. Tennis is a physical activity that has specific rules and allows students to make direct observations. Once they collect enough data, they can make an experimental prediction and study the results.

5. *Students will be able to test what will happen to water if the surrounding temperature changes.*

   This statement is an example of experimenting. Water changing its state of matter is a physical phenomenon and can be directly observed.

6. *Students will be able to select the most suitable format for a persuasive essay based on specific criteria.*

   This statement is an example of decision making. Students must determine which format will best support a persuasive essay using specific criteria to make their decisions.

7. *Students will be able to research and take a position on a current political issue.*

   This statement is an example of investigating. Because there is no absolutely correct or incorrect position to take on a political issue, students can use only actions, opinions, and events from which to gather information. They must develop a logical argument as opposed to an argument based on empirical evidence.

8. *Students will be able to determine the probability of a specific outcome given a set of conditions.*

   This statement is an example of problem solving. Because specified conditions exist, students must overcome a hurdle before reaching the right answer—they must solve a problem.

9. *Students will be able to develop a strategy for collecting data schoolwide given a limited period of time.*

   This statement is an example of problem solving. The parameters of area and time present the students not only with a task, but also with an obstacle to overcome in order to accomplish that task.

10. *Students will be able to research and make a presentation on the life of an influential American leader.*

    This statement is an example of investigating. In this case, students are examining the life of a person, not observing a physical activity or event.

Answers to Exercise 4.1

Ordering Goals by Level of Difficulty

The correct order for the learning goals appears in order from most difficult to least difficult.

A. *Students will be able to discuss what would happen to the body if one of its needs was not met.* Because this goal requires students to make a prediction, the level of cognition involved is specifying, which is a form of analysis.

Students will be able to discuss the body's most important dietary needs. Students are being asked to determine which of the body's needs are most important. They must be able to understand, for example, that water is a more immediate and important need than clothing. In order to accomplish this goal, students must use integration, a component of comprehension.

Students will be able to recognize healthy versus unhealthy foods given a list. The goal states that a list of foods is provided to the student; therefore, recognition (retrieval) is being employed. The student is not being asked to produce information or distinguish between facts.

B. *Students will be able to design complex word problems based on given mathematical equations.* This goal requires the execution of a complex procedure. Not only must students understand equations, they must also be able to design problems based on them.

Students will be able to translate between simple word problems and mathematical equations. This goal requires the execution of a procedure that is simpler than the preceding procedure because there is no element of design.

Students will be able to recognize accurate statements about the mathematical processes embedded in word problems. This goal involves retrieval; the student must pick out correct statements provided about the mathematical processes involved in a word problem.

C. *Students will be able to combine simple, compound, and compound-complex sentences fluently.* Although this goal involves only execution, it is the most difficult of the set because it requires the highest level of execution. Stringing sentences of varied structure together is more complex than writing either simple or complex sentences in isolation.

Students will be able to write compound-complex sentences in isolation. This goal requires execution. Writing compound-complex sentences is a more difficult execution than writing simple sentences, and it is simpler than writing multiple sentences with varied structure.

Designing and Teaching Learning Goals and Objectives • © 2009 Marzano Research Laboratory • marzanoresearch.com
Visit **marzanoresearch.com/classroomstrategies** to download this page.

Students will be able to write a simple sentence with a subject and a predicate. Execution is the essence of this goal as writing always involves the performing of a procedure. This execution is the simplest of the group because it only requires students to write a simple sentence.

D. *Students will be able to convert between standard and nonstandard unit measurements.* This goal requires execution of the most complex procedure of the set of procedures. Students must have enough knowledge of both standard and nonstandard units to be able to make conversions between systems. For example, students might be asked to determine how many feet are in a meter or how many centimeters are in a foot.

Students will be able to make simple conversions within standard or nonstandard unit measurements. This goal requires the execution of a more complex procedure than the following goal and a simpler procedure than the preceding goal. Students might be able to determine how many inches are in three feet or how many feet are in a mile.

Students will be able to make simple measurements in standard units. This goal requires execution of a simple procedure that involves standard units only.

E. *Students will be able to compare the successes and failures of different presidents' foreign policies during times of conflict.* This goal requires matching, a component of analysis, in that it requires students to find similarities and differences between the foreign policies of different presidents during times of conflict. It is the most complex goal in the set because it is at the analysis level.

Students will be able to discuss the key aspects of Roosevelt's foreign policy during World War II. This goal requires integration (comprehension). Students must have enough of an understanding of Roosevelt's foreign policy during World War II to discuss its key aspects.

Students will be able to recognize accurate statements about Roosevelt's foreign policy during World War II. This goal is the simplest of the set because it only requires students to employ retrieval by recognizing accurate statements that have been provided.

Designing and Teaching Learning Goals and Objectives • © 2009 Marzano Research Laboratory • marzanoresearch.com
Visit **marzanoresearch.com/classroomstrategies** to download this page.

Answers to Exercise 4.2 (Designing a Scale) will vary.

Score 4.0	The student:
	•
	No major errors or omissions regarding the score 4.0 content
Score 3.5	In addition to score 3.0 performance, partial success at score 4.0 content
Score 3.0	The student:
	•
	No major errors or omissions regarding the score 3.0 content
Score 2.5	No major errors or omissions regarding score 2.0 content, and partial success at score 3.0 content
Score 2.0	The student:
	•
	No major errors or omissions regarding the score 2.0 content
Score 1.5	Partial success at score 2.0 content, but major errors or omissions regarding score 3.0 content
Score 1.0	**With help, partial success at score 2.0 content and score 3.0 content**
Score 0.5	With help, partial success at score 2.0 content, but not at score 3.0 content
Score 0.0	**Even with help, no success**

Answers to Exercise 4.3

Designing Noncognitive Scales

1. *Target (score 3.0) goal: The student discusses the consequences for breaking home and classroom rules.*

   This might be considered a self-awareness/self-control goal. Though this goal may seem to involve analysis because it asks students to determine what would happen given a particular situation (breaking the rules), it is actually just asking for recall (retrieval of information). Most classroom and home rules are explicitly stated, as are the consequences for breaking those rules, so students have only to recall what they have been told in order to accomplish the goal. A simpler goal would require students to recognize accurate statements about class and home rules and the consequences for breaking them. A more complex goal might ask students to create a generalization, based on their knowledge of class and home rules, about what kinds of behaviors might be appropriate and inappropriate in outside situations such as restaurants, churches, or libraries.

2. *Target (score 3.0) goal: The student picks up on and utilizes appropriate nonverbal language.*

   This might be considered a social awareness and response goal. It requires an awareness of a student's own emotions and the emotions of others as they are revealed through nonverbal language. It asks students to demonstrate integration in that they must be able to determine which actions constitute nonverbal language and which do not, and it requires execution in that it asks students to not only understand relevant nonverbal language, but to use it. A simpler goal (score 2.0) might ask students to use a retrieval process such as: *The student recognizes or recalls accurate statements about or isolated examples of nonverbal language.* A more complex goal might involve a discussion of possible misunderstandings that can arise based on misreading nonverbal language, which would be an error analysis process.

3. *Target (score 3.0) goal: The student includes others in class assignments or games.*

   This goal might fall under the topic of empathy/respect. It asks students to have enough awareness of and concern for others to include them in group activities. This effort would be classified as execution. A simpler goal (score 2.0) might involve retrieval of information about the process of including others, such as: *The student recognizes or recalls accurate statements about the value of including others.* A more complex goal (score 4.0) might involve a higher level of execution, which could be something like: *The student stands up for fellow students who are being picked on or bullied.* A score 4.0 goal could also ask students for some kind of analysis: *The student discusses a time when he or she failed to include someone and what he or she could have done differently.*

APPENDIX B

WHAT IS AN EFFECT SIZE?

Reports on educational research use terms such as *meta-analysis* and *effect size* (ES). While these terms are without doubt useful to researchers, they can be confusing and even frustrating for the practitioner. So what does meta-analysis mean exactly? What is an effect size?

A meta-analysis is a summary, or synthesis, of relevant research findings. It looks at all of the individual studies done on a particular topic and summarizes them. This is helpful to educators in that a meta-analysis provides more and stronger support than does a single analysis (meta-analysis is literally an analysis of analyses).

An average effect size tells us about the results across all of the individual studies examined. For example, let's say the purpose of the meta-analysis is to examine multiple studies regarding the effect of clear learning goals on student achievement (that is, the effect of X on Y). An average effect size reports the results of all of the included studies to tell us whether or not clear learning goals improve student achievement and, if so, by how much.

Exactly how does a meta-analysis work, and how is an effect size calculated? Empirical research is highly detailed and often uses idiomatic language; however, in the following steps we have made efforts to demystify the processes of meta-analysis and effect size calculation.

1. *Researchers survey the wide field of educational studies available with an eye for what is relevant to their meta-analysis.* They create keyword lists to help determine the breadth and depth of the search. Published articles, nonpublished articles, dissertations, book chapters, and online and other electronic databases are considered for inclusion. Quite simply, they construct a database of all relevant studies.

2. *After an initial examination of the relevant studies, researchers have an idea of the rigor of each study. They craft their own inclusion criteria by asking which studies are good enough to include and which studies should be excluded.* They also pay close attention to the similarities and differences between the studies. Strong results will be based on

meta-analyses that use studies with common purposes and variables. In other words, researchers want to include the studies that are most analogous. For example, if one study defines student achievement in terms of standardized test scores, and another defines student achievement in terms of students' self-reported learning, researchers would probably not include both studies in the same meta-analysis.

3. *Once researchers have identified the studies they will use for a meta-analysis, they examine the results of each study.* Specifically, they look at the effect sizes of each study in order to mathematically calculate an average effect size (ES) for the overall meta-analysis.

The process behind calculating the ES is quite detailed, but basically, it is computed by determining the difference between the mean of the experimental group (the group that has had the benefit of a particular educational practice), and the mean of the control group (the group that has not had the benefit of a particular educational practice), and then dividing the difference by the standard deviation. In simple terms, a standard deviation is the average distance each score is from the mean. For example, if the mean of a group of scores is 60, and the standard deviation is 5, then the average distance each score is from 60 is 5.

To illustrate how an effect size is computed, let's assume that one class of science students is the experimental group; their class received clear learning goals and took a test on the science content addressed during a specific unit. Another class served as the control group; those students did not receive clear learning goals for that unit and took the same test. The experimental group had a mean (average) score of 85 on the test, and the control group had a mean score of 75. The standard deviation for the test given to both groups was 20. The effect size for this study would be .50 [(85 − 75)/ 20]. This means that the average score in the experimental group is .50 of a standard deviation larger than the mean score of the control group.

An advantage of the effect size is that it can be readily and accurately interpreted in terms of average percentile gain. A percentile gain effectively translates an effect size into a language we can understand. Just how this is done requires a somewhat detailed explanation. Briefly though, an effect size is equivalent to a point on the normal distribution, and once you have a point on the normal distribution, you can determine the expected percentile gain (or loss) for someone at the 50th percentile. Table A.1 lists expected percentile gains for various effect sizes.

If the effect size for use of clear learning goals is .50, for example, a teacher could predict that students in the classroom will improve by 19 percentile points. That is, students scoring at the 50th percentile on achievement tests would be predicted to score at the 69th percentile after clear learning goals had been introduced. In general, the higher the effect size, the better.

When an average effect size is calculated using a number of studies in a meta-analysis, practitioners can be even more sure that the average effect size and its associated percentile gain will be found in classes where the specific educational practice that is the focus of a meta-analysis is being used.

Although terms such as *meta-analysis, average effect size*, and *percentile gain* may look daunting at first, they are ultimately employed to gather the widest array of the strongest research and translate the findings into meaningful language for the classroom teacher or school administrator.

Table A.1 Conversion of Effect Size to Percentile Gain

Effect Size	Percentile Gain	Effect Size	Percentile Gain	Effect Size	Percentile Gain	Effect Size	Percentile Gain
		0.5	19	1	34	1.5	43
0.01	0	0.51	19	1.01	34	1.51	43
0.02	1	0.52	20	1.02	35	1.52	44
0.03	1	0.53	20	1.03	35	1.53	44
0.04	2	0.54	21	1.04	35	1.54	44
0.05	2	0.55	21	1.05	35	1.55	44
0.06	2	0.56	21	1.06	36	1.56	44
0.07	3	0.57	22	1.07	36	1.57	44
0.08	3	0.58	22	1.08	36	1.58	44
0.09	4	0.59	22	1.09	36	1.59	44
0.1	4	0.6	23	1.1	36	1.6	45
0.11	4	0.61	23	1.11	37	1.61	45
0.12	5	0.62	23	1.12	37	1.62	45
0.13	5	0.63	24	1.13	37	1.63	45
0.14	6	0.64	24	1.14	37	1.64	45
0.15	6	0.65	24	1.15	37	1.65	45
0.16	6	0.66	25	1.16	38	1.66	45
0.17	7	0.67	25	1.17	38	1.67	45
0.18	7	0.68	25	1.18	38	1.68	45
0.19	8	0.69	25	1.19	38	1.69	45
0.2	8	0.7	26	1.2	38	1.7	46
0.21	8	0.71	26	1.21	39	1.71	46
0.22	9	0.72	26	1.22	39	1.72	46
0.23	9	0.73	27	1.23	39	1.73	46
0.24	9	0.74	27	1.24	39	1.74	46
0.25	10	0.75	27	1.25	39	1.75	46

Continued on next page →

Effect Size	Percentile Gain	Effect Size	Percentile Gain	Effect Size	Percentile Gain	Effect Size	Percentile Gain
0.26	10	0.76	28	1.26	40	1.76	46
0.27	11	0.77	28	1.27	40	1.77	46
0.28	11	0.78	28	1.28	40	1.78	46
0.29	11	0.79	29	1.29	40	1.79	46
0.3	12	0.8	29	1.3	40	1.8	46
0.31	12	0.81	29	1.31	40	1.81	46
0.32	13	0.82	29	1.32	41	1.82	47
0.33	13	0.83	30	1.33	41	1.83	47
0.34	13	0.84	30	1.34	41	1.84	47
0.35	14	0.85	30	1.35	41	1.85	47
0.36	14	0.86	31	1.36	41	1.86	47
0.37	14	0.87	31	1.37	41	1.87	47
0.38	15	0.88	31	1.38	42	1.88	47
0.39	15	0.89	31	1.39	42	1.89	47
0.4	16	0.9	32	1.4	42	1.9	47
0.41	16	0.91	32	1.41	42	1.91	47
0.42	16	0.92	32	1.42	42	1.92	47
0.43	17	0.93	32	1.43	42	1.93	47
0.44	17	0.94	33	1.44	43	1.94	47
0.45	17	0.95	33	1.45	43	1.95	47
0.46	18	0.96	33	1.46	43	1.96	48
0.47	18	0.97	33	1.47	43	1.97	48
0.48	18	0.98	34	1.48	43	1.98	48
0.49	19	0.99	34	1.49	43	1.99	48

Note: Effect sizes over 2.00 correspond to percentile gains of 49%.

APPENDIX C

TERMS AND PHRASES FROM THE NEW TAXONOMY

Level of Difficulty	Mental Process	Terms and Phrases
Level 4 Knowledge Utilization	Decision Making	Decide
		Select the best among the following alternatives
		Which among the following would be the best
		What is the best way
		Which of these is most suitable
	Problem Solving	Solve
		How would you overcome
		Adapt
		Develop a strategy to
		Figure out a way to
		How will you reach your goal under these conditions
	Experimenting	Experiment
		Generate and test
		Test the idea that
		What would happen if
		How would you test that
		How would you determine if
		How can this be explained
		Based on the experiment, what can be predicted
	Investigating	Investigate
		Research
		Find out about
		Take a position on
		What are the differing features of
		How did this happen
		Why did this happen
		What would have happened if
Level 3 Analysis	Matching	Categorize
		Compare and contrast
		Differentiate
		Discriminate
		Distinguish
		Sort
		Create an analogy
		Create a metaphor
	Classifying	Classify
		Organize
		Sort
		Identify a broader category
		Identify categories
		Identify different types

Level of Difficulty	Mental Process	Terms and Phrases
	Analyzing Errors	Identify errors
		Identify problems
		Identify issues
		Identify misunderstandings
		Assess
		Critique
		Diagnose
		Evaluate
		Edit
		Revise
	Generalizing	Generalize
		What conclusions can be drawn
		What inferences can be made
		Create a generalization
		Create a principle
		Create a rule
		Trace the development of
		Form conclusions
	Specifying	Make and defend
		Predict
		Judge
		Deduce
		What would have to happen
		Develop an argument for
		Under what conditions
Level 2 Comprehension	Integrating	Describe how or why
		Describe the key parts of
		Describe the effects
		Describe the relationship between
		Explain ways in which
		Paraphrase
		Summarize
	Symbolizing	Symbolize
		Depict
		Represent
		Illustrate
		Draw
		Show
		Use models
		Diagram
		Chart

Continued on next page →

Level of Difficulty	Mental Process	Terms and Phrases
Level 1 Retrieval	Recognizing	Recognize (from a list)
		Select from (a list)
		Identify (from a list)
		Determine (if the following statements are true)
	Recalling	Exemplify
		Name
		List
		Label
		State
		Describe
		Identify who
		Describe what
		Identify where
		Identify when
	Executing	Use
		Demonstrate
		Show
		Make
		Complete
		Draft

REFERENCES

Abedi, J., & O'Neil, H. F. (2005). Assessment of noncognitive influences on learning. *Educational Assessment, 10*(3), 147–151.

Anderson, L. W., Krathwohl, D. R., Airasian, P. W., Cruikshank, K. A., Mayer, R. E., Pintrich, P. R., et al. (Eds.). (2001). *A taxonomy for learning, teaching, and assessing: A revision of Bloom's taxonomy of educational objectives.* New York: Longman.

Aronson, E., Blaney, N., Stephan, C., Sikes, J., & Snapp, M. (1978). *The jigsaw classroom.* Beverley Hills, CA: Sage.

Azevedo, R., & Bernard, R. M. (1995). A meta-analysis of the effects of feedback in computer-based instruction. *Journal of Educational Computing Research, 13*(2), 109–125.

Bangert-Drowns, R. L., Kulik, C. C., Kulik, J. A., & Morgan, M. (1991). The instructional effects of feedback in test-like events. *Review of Educational Research, 61*(2), 213–238.

Bloom, B. S. (1976). *Human characteristics and school learning.* New York: McGraw-Hill.

Bowen, C.W. (2000). A quantitative review of cooperative learning effects on high school and college chemistry achievement. *Journal of Chemical Education, 77*(1), 116–119.

Burns, M. K. (2004). Empirical analysis of drill ratio research: Refining the instructional level for drill tasks. *Remedial and Special Education, 25*(3), 167–173.

Chidester, T. R., & Grigsby, W. C. (1984). A meta-analysis of the goal setting-performance literature. *Academy of Management Proceedings*, 202–206.

Donovan, J. J., & Radosevich, D. J. (1998). The moderating role of goal commitment on the goal difficulty-performance relationship: A meta-analytic review and critical reanalysis. *Journal of Applied Psychology, 83*(2), 308–315.

Durlak, J. A., & Weissberg, R. P. (2007). *The impact of after-school programs that promote personal and social skills.* Chicago: Collaborative for Academic, Social, and Emotional Learning.

Fuchs, L. S., & Fuchs, D. (1985). *The effect of measuring student progress toward long vs. short-term goals: A meta-analysis.* (ERIC Document Reproduction Service No. ED263142) Accessed at www.eric.ed.gov on April 8, 2009.

Ginsburg-Block, M. D., Rohrbeck, C. A., & Fantuzzo, J. W. (2006). A meta-analytic review of social, self-concept, and behavioral outcomes of peer-assisted learning. *Journal of Educational Psychology, 98*(4), 732–749.

Gollwitzer, P. M., & Sheeran, P. (2006). Implementation intentions and goal achievement: A meta-analysis of effects and processes. *Advances in Experimental Social Psychology, 38,* 69–119.

Graham, S., & Perin, D. (2007). *Writing next: Effective strategies to improve writing of adolescents in middle and high schools—A report to Carnegie Corporation of New York.* Washington DC: Alliance for Excellent Education. Accessed at www.all4ed.org/publications/WritingNext/WritingNext.pdf on January 24, 2009.

Haas, M. (2005). Teaching methods for secondary algebra: A meta-analysis of findings. *NASSP Bulletin, 89*(642), 24–46.

Hall, L. E. (1989). The effects of cooperative learning on achievement: A meta-analysis. *Dissertation Abstracts International, 50,* 343A. (UMI No. 8910420)

Haller, E. P., Child, D. A., & Walberg, H. J. (1998). Can comprehension be taught? A quantitative synthesis of "metacognitive studies." *Educational Researcher, 17*(9), 5–8.

Hattie, J. A. (1999, August). *Influences on student learning.* Inaugural professorial address, University of Auckland, New Zealand. Accessed at www.teacherstoolbox.co.uk/downloads/managers/Influencesonstudent.pdf on January 24, 2009.

Hattie, J. A. (2009). *Visible learning: A synthesis of over 800 meta-analyses relating to achievement.* New York: Routledge.

Hattie, J. A., & Timperley, H. (2007). The power of feedback. *Review of Educational Research, 77*(1), 81–112.

Johnson, D. W., & Johnson, R. T. (1989). *Cooperation and competition: Theory and research.* Edina, MN: Interaction Book Company.

Johnson, D. W., & Johnson, R. T. (1999). *Learning together and alone: Cooperative, competitive, and individualistic learning.* Boston: Allyn & Bacon.

Johnson, D. W., Johnson, R. T., & Holubec, E. (1998). *Cooperation in the classroom* (6th ed.). Edina, MN: Interaction Book Company.

Johnson, D. W., Maruyama, G., Johnson, R. T., Nelson, D., & Skon, L. (1981). Effects of cooperative, competitive, and individualistic goal structures on achievement: A meta-analysis. *Psychological Bulletin, 89*(1), 47–62.

Kaplan, A., Middleton, M. J., Urdan, T., & Midgley, C. (2001). Achievement goals and goal structures. In C. Midgley (Ed.), *Goals, goal structures, and patterns of adaptive learning* (pp. 21–54). Hillsdale, NJ: Lawrence Erlbaum.

King, A., Staffieri, A., & Adelgais, A. (1998). Mutual peer tutoring: Effects of structuring tutorial interaction to scaffold peer learning. *Journal of Educational Psychology, 90,* 134–152.

Klein, H. J., Wesson, M. J., Hollenbeck, J. R., & Alge, B. J. (1999). Goal commitment and the goal-setting process: Conceptual clarification and empirical synthesis. *Journal of Applied Psychology, 84*(6), 885–896.

Kluger, A. N., & DeNisi, A. (1996). The effects of feedback interventions on performance: A historical review, a meta-analysis, and a preliminary feedback intervention theory. *Psychological Bulletin, 119*(2), 254–284.

Krajcik, J., McNeill, K. L., & Reiser, B. J. (2007). Learning-goals-driven design model: Developing curriculum materials that align with national standards and incorporate project-based pedagogy. *Science Education, 92*(1), 1–32.

Krathwohl, D. R., & Payne, D. A. (1971). Defining and assessing educational objectives. In R. L. Thorndike (Ed.), *Educational measurement* (pp. 17–45). Washington, DC: American Council on Education.

Kumar, D. D. (1991). A meta-analysis of the relationship between science instruction and student engagement. *Education Review, 43*(1), 49–66.

Lipsey, M. W., & Wilson, D. B. (1993). The efficacy of psychological, educational, and behavioral treatment. *American Psychologist, 48*(12), 1181–1209.

Locke, E. A., & Latham, G. P. (1990). *A theory of goal setting and task performance.* Englewood Cliffs, NJ: Prentice Hall.

Locke, E. A., & Latham, G. P. (2002). Building a practically useful theory of goal setting and task motivation. *American Psychologist, 57*(9), 705–717.

Lysakowski, R. S., & Walberg, H. J. (1981). Classroom reinforcement in relation to learning: A quantitative analysis. *Journal of Educational Research, 75*, 69–77.

Lysakowski, R. S., & Walberg, H. J. (1982). Instructional effects of cues, participation, and corrective feedback: A quantitative synthesis. *American Educational Research Journal, 19*(4), 559–578.

Mager, R. F. (1962). *Preparing instructional objectives.* Palo Alto, CA: Fearon.

Marzano, R. J. (2006). *Classroom assessment and grading that work.* Alexandria, VA: Association for Supervision and Curriculum Development.

Marzano, R. J. (2007). *The art and science of teaching: A comprehensive framework for effective instruction.* Alexandria, VA: Association for Supervision and Curriculum Development.

Marzano, R. J. (in press). *Formative assessment and standards-based grading: The classroom strategies series.* Bloomington, IN: Marzano Research Laboratory.

Marzano, R. J., & Haystead, M. W. (2008). *Making standards useful in the classroom.* Alexandria, VA: Association for Supervision and Curriculum Development.

Marzano, R. J., & Kendall, J. S. (2007). *The new taxonomy of educational objectives* (2nd ed.). Thousand Oaks, CA: Corwin Press.

Marzano, R. J., & Kendall, J. S. (2008). *Designing & assessing educational objectives: Applying the new taxonomy.* Thousand Oaks, CA: Corwin Press.

Marzano, R. J., Marzano, J. S., & Pickering, D. J. (2003). *Classroom management that works: Research-based strategies for every teacher.* Alexandria, VA: Association for Supervision and Curriculum Development.

Marzano, R. J., Pickering, D. J., & Pollock, J. (2001). *Classroom instruction that works*. Alexandria, VA: Association for Supervision and Curriculum Development.

Meece, J. L. (1991). The classroom context and students' motivational goals. In M. L. Maehr & P. R. Pintrich (Eds.), *Advances in motivation and achievement: A research annual* (Vol. 7) (pp. 261–285). Greenwich, CT: JAI Press.

Mento, A. J., Steel, R. P., & Karren, R. J. (1987). A meta-analytic study of the effects of goal setting on task performance: 1966–1984. *Organizational Behavior and Human Decision Processes, 39*(1), 52–83.

Moin, A. K. (1986). *Relative effectiveness of various techniques of calculus instruction: A meta-analysis.* Unpublished doctoral dissertation, Department of Mathematics, University of Syracuse, New York.

O'Donnell, A. M. (2006). The role of peers and group learning. In P. Alexander & P. Winne (Eds.), *Handbook of Educational Psychology* (2nd ed., pp. 781–802). Mahwah, NJ: Lawrence Erlbaum.

Roseth, C. J., Johnson, D. W., & Johnson, R. T. (2008). Promoting early adolescents' achievement and peer relationships: The effects of cooperative, competitive, and individualistic goal structures. *Psychological Bulletin, 134*(2), 223–246.

Sharan, S., & Hertz-Lazarowitz, R. (1980). A group investigation method of cooperative learning in the classroom. In S. Sharan, P. Hare, C. Webb, & R. Hertz-Lazarowitz (Eds.), *Cooperation in education* (pp. 14–46). Provo, UT: Brigham Young University Press.

Tenenbaum, G., & Goldring, E. (1989). A meta-analysis of the effect of enhanced instruction: Cues, participation, reinforcement, and feedback and correctives on motor skill learning. *Journal of Research and Development in Education, 22*(3), 53–64.

Tomlinson, C. A. (1999). *The differentiated classroom: Responding to the needs of all learners*. Alexandria, VA: Association for Supervision and Curriculum Development.

Tomlinson, C. A. (2004). *How to differentiate instruction in mixed-ability classrooms* (2nd ed.). Alexandria, VA: Association for Supervision and Curriculum Development.

Tubbs, M. E. (1986). Goal setting: A meta-analytic examination of the empirical evidence. *Journal of Applied Psychology, 71*(3), 474–483.

Tyler, R. W. (1949a). *Basic principles of curriculum and instruction*. Chicago: University of Chicago Press.

Tyler, R. W. (1949b). *Constructing achievement tests*. Chicago: University of Chicago Press.

Utman, C. H. (1997). Performance effects of motivational state: A meta-analysis. *Personality and Social Psychology Review, 1*(2), 170–182.

Valentine, J. C., DuBois, D. L., & Cooper, H. (2004). The relation between self-beliefs and academic achievement: A meta-analytic review. *Educational Psychologist, 39*(2), 111–133.

Walberg, H. J. (1999). Productive teaching. In H. C. Waxman & H. J. Walberg (Eds.), *New directions for teaching practice and research* (pp. 75–104). Berkeley, CA: McCutchen.

Wise, K. C., & Okey, J. R. (1983). A meta-analysis of the effects of various science teaching strategies on achievement. *Journal of Research in Science Teaching, 20*(5), 415–425.

Wood, R. E., Mento, A. J., & Locke, E. A. (1987). Task complexity as a moderator of goal effects: A meta-analysis. *Journal of Applied Psychology, 72*(3), 416–425.

Wright, P. M. (1990). Operationalization of goal difficulty as a moderator of the goal difficulty-performance relationship. *Journal of Applied Psychology, 75*(3), 227–234.

Yeany, R. H., & Miller, P. A. (1983). Effects of diagnostic/remedial instruction on science learning: A meta-analysis. *Journal of Research in Science Teaching, 20*, 19–26.

INDEX